HOW TO PASS THE
LIFE IN THE
UK TEST

“ To settle in the UK and to pass the Life in the UK Test you will need a solid understanding of English, as well as many of the processes involved in living within the British Isles. *How to pass the Life in the UK Test* will help you through this process. **”**

HOW TO PASS THE LIFE IN THE UK TEST

Which? Books are commissioned and published by Which? Ltd,
2 Marylebone Road, London NW1 4DF
Email: books@which.co.uk

Distributed by Littlehampton Book Services Ltd, Faraday Close, Durrington, Worthing,
West Sussex BN13 3RB

British Library Cataloguing in Publication Data
A catalogue record for this book is available from the British Library

Chapters 2–7 from *Life in the United Kingdom: A Journey to Citizenship* 2007
(Second Edition, 978 0 11 341313 3)
Copyright © Crown copyright 2007
Reproduced under the terms of the Click-Use Licence

All other text copyright © Which? Ltd 2009

ISBN 978 1 84490 058 9

1 3 5 7 9 10 8 6 4 2

The Life in the UK Test questions are currently based exclusively on the text contained
within Chapters 2–6 of the second edition of the official Home Office guide, *Life in
the United Kingdom: A Journey to Citizenship*. This text is reproduced verbatim here,
in Chapters 2–6 of this guide. To help you revise the information, we have devised
a series of practice questions. These are not the official questions, nor are they a
substitute for reading the chapters, but they are designed to help you prepare for the
actual questions by testing you on the same material and using the same approach.

Project manager: Claudia Dyer
Edited by: Victoria Walker
Designed by: Philip Jansseune for Walker Jansseune
Index by: Lynda Swindells
Cover images by: iStockphoto Images
Printed and bound by: Stanley L Hunt (Printers) Ltd., Northamptonshire.

This book is printed on UPM Fine manufactured by UPM -Kymmene. The mill is ISO
14001 and EMAS certified. UPM Fine is Elemental Chlorine Free, is sourced from
Sustainable Forests, and is both PEFC and FSC certified.

For a full list of Which? Books, please call 01903 828557, access our website at
www.which.co.uk, or write to Littlehampton Book Services. For other enquiries call
0800 252 100.

Contents

Introduction

The need to show an understanding of the language and life in the UK
was first introduced as part of the naturalisation process in November 2005.
In April 2007, the requirement to take a language and citizenship test or
course was extended to include anyone seeking indefinite leave to remain.

ABOUT THIS GUIDE

This book is designed to help you study and pass the Life in the UK Test.
In addition to reproducing the official Home Office text on which the test
is based, it provides background information on the test and study tips.
There are also nearly 400 practice test questions contained in this book,
and 1,000 on the accompanying CD–ROM. These are not the official
questions, but are designed to help you prepare for the actual questions
by testing you on the same material and using the same approach.

KNOWLEDGE OF LANGUAGE AND LIFE IN THE UK

The Life in the UK Test is an integral part of the UK's naturalisation
process. When it was first introduced, the Home Office explained that it
wanted to create a new, more meaningful, way of becoming a citizen in
an effort to help people integrate and share in British values and traditions.
Now everyone who wishes to be granted indefinite leave to remain in
the UK and everyone who applies for British citizenship must prove their
knowledge of language and life in the UK. There are two ways you
can do this. You must either pass the test, or pass a course on English
language and citizenship. If you can speak English well enough, you only
need to take the test.

If you do not speak English, you will need to study the English
language and citizenship course, known as ESOL. This stands for English
for Speakers of Other Languages. The course is divided into three levels:

- ESOL Entry 1
- ESOL Entry 2
- ESOL Entry 3

Your course tutor will assess at which level you need to begin. If you are not sure about whether you should study the ESOL course or take the test, contact your local ESOL study centre. A course supervisor will assess you and advise you on the best route for you. Alternatively, you could try working your way through the navigational tutorial on the Life in the UK Test website (www.lifeintheuktest.gov.uk). If you find this difficult to understand, it would be wise for you to enrol on one of the ESOL courses. There is normally a charge applied to studying an ESOL course, although these can vary between colleges. Contact your local college for details of their fees.

> **❝If you are not sure about whether you should study the ESOL course or take the test, contact your local ESOL study centre.❞**

BACKGROUND TO THE TEST

Prior to the introduction of the Life in the UK Test, becoming a citizen of the UK was largely a bureaucratic process. However, a decision was made to move the focus away from form-filling and hurdle-leaping. Instead, an important component of becoming a citizen would be the enhancement of skills and knowledge that would make settling in the UK much easier.

An advisory group chaired by Sir Bernard Crick, who had previously chaired a similar group looking into adding 'citizenship' into the state schools' curriculum, was set up. This group proposed that English language skills and a knowledge of life in the UK were vital for achieving economic, civic and social integration. The work of this group led to the introduction of the Life in the UK Test and language and citizenship classes.

To find a local college that offers courses in English for Speakers of Other Languages (ESOL) and citizenship, contact Learn Direct. See www.learndirect.co.uk or call their helpline on 0800 100 900.

TEST EXEMPTIONS

Some citizenship applicants are exempt from having to demonstrate their knowledge of language and life in the UK. These include:

- Anyone under the age of 18 or over the age of 65 (you will need to remember to send your passport or birth certificate as proof of your age with your application);
- Anyone who has a long-term illness or disability that restricts their ability to attend the language classes or the test;
- Anyone who has a mental impairment that prevents them from being able to learn another language or pass a test.

If a disability provides you with a valid exemption, you will need to send evidence from a qualified medical practitioner confirming your disability when you submit your citizenship application.

Further exemptions from the test and course apply to certain categories of people applying for permanent residence. These include citizens and their spouses or civil partners of other countries who are on discharge from HM Forces. It also includes the civil partners and spouses of British citizens. For a full list of these exemptions, see the website of the UK Border Agency. However, even if you fulfil the exemption criteria for permanent residence, if you subsequently wish to apply for citizenship, you will then need to pass the test or course in the same way as any other citizenship applicant.

CITIZENSHIP APPLICATION ADVICE

For specific or legal advice on your own application for British citizenship, you must speak to a qualified, registered adviser. All immigration advisers must be registered with the Office of Immigrations Services Commissioner or an agency such as the Citizens Advice Bureau. It is a criminal offence to offer immigration advice without such registration.

To find a solicitor who specialises in immigration work, contact the Immigration Law Practitioners' Association. Most law centres also have a specialist in immigration who may be able to advise you for free. To find a

 For further information about who should sit the Life in the UK Test and who has an exemption, see the website of the Home Office's UK Border Agency at www.ukba.homeoffice.gov.uk or call the Immigration Agency Enquiry Bureau on 0870 606 7766.

law centre near you, contact the Law Centres' Federation or the Scottish Association of Law Centres, or Law Centre Northern Ireland.

The Immigration Advisory Service (IAS) is a charitable organisation that offers free immigration advice and representation to people who are entitled to legal aid. It also provides a fee-paying service for people who are not entitled to legal aid.

❝ For specific or legal advice on your own application for British citizenship, you must speak to a qualified, registered adviser. ❞

The UK Border Agency runs a Nationality Contact Centre. This provides advice on British citizenship and right of abode. It is open weekdays from 9am to 9pm. It tends to experience a high volume of calls and you might find it better to ring during the evening when the centre is less busy.

Citizenship application advisers

The UK Border Agency Nationality Contact Centre
Tel: 0845 010 5200

Immigration Law Practitioners' Association (ILPA)
Tel: 020 7251 8383
Website: www.ilpa.org.uk

Law Centres' Federation (LCF)
Tel: 020 7428 4400
Website: www.lawcentres.org.uk

Scottish Association of Law Centres (SALC)
Tel: 0141 440 2503
Website: www.govanloc.com/salc

Law Centre Northern Ireland
Tel: 028 9024 4401
Website: www.lawcentreni.org

The Citizens Advice Bureau (CAB)
Website: www.citizensadviceorg.uk

Immigration Advisory Service (IAS)
Tel: 0844 974 4000
Website: www.iasuk.org

“Although they can't give you advice on your application, many local authorities provide a nationality checking service. ”

In addition, although they can't give you advice on your application, many local authorities provide a nationality checking service. This service enables you to make your application for British citizenship in person at your local council offices. Although this incurs an additional fee (the amount is set by the local authority and varies around the country), the council staff will check with you that you have completed the paperwork correctly. This includes checking:

- The application form has been filled out correctly
- You have provided all of the necessary supporting documents
- You have included the correct fee.

> **!** The second edition of the Home Office official guide, *Life in the United Kingdom: A Journey to Citizenship*, was published in March 2007. Since then, there have been a number of Government initiatives and legislation which have subsequently dated parts of the official study material.
> For example, the minimum wage has risen three times since the figures published in this edition. Throughout this book, we will let you know where current law or policy differs from that discussed in the official text. However, it is important to remember that you will be tested on the text contained in the official Home Office guide (Chapters 2-6 of this book), not on the latest legislation.

HOW TO USE THIS BOOK

The Life in the UK Test questions are currently based exclusively on the text contained within Chapters 2-6 of the second edition of the official Home Office guide, *Life in the United Kingdom: A Journey to Citizenship*. This text is reproduced verbatim here, in Chapters 2-6 of this Which? Essential Guide, *How to Pass the Life in the UK Test*. To pass the test, you must understand and be able to recall the material contained in these chapters.

To help you revise the information contained in these chapters, we have devised a series of practice questions. These are not the official Life in the UK Test questions, nor are they a substitute for reading the chapters. Practising them alone will not be enough to prepare you adequately for the real test.

❝ By studying the relevant chapters in this book and using the practice test CD-ROM, we are confident that you will be well on the way to passing the test. ❞

HOW TO USE THE CD-ROM – PRACTICE QUESTIONS

Included with this book is a CD-ROM which contains a series of mock tests. Each time you take a test you will be given 24 random questions from the extensive database of questions and answers. This is designed to echo the real test, which also contains 24 questions.

However, the practice questions and answers will not be exactly the same as you get in the actual test. They are designed to represent the sort of questions that the test contains.

By studying the relevant chapters in this book and using the practice test CD-ROM, we are confident that you will be well on the way to passing the test.

 For further information on how to use the CD-ROM, see pages 19 to 24.

Although similar to the actual test you will need to take, the CD-ROM also contains some significant differences. For example, the Which? CD-ROM practice tests will provide you with a summary of your test results, including which questions you answered incorrectly. When you take the real Life in the UK Test, the test supervisor will inform you whether you have passed or failed. However, you will not be told which answers you got right and wrong.

In addition to providing you with the answers to questions, the CD-ROM will also provide you with an example of the text on which each question is based. The actual Life in the UK Test does not offer any such clues. The Life in the UK computer test will offer you the option of hearing each question. The CD-ROM does not contain an audio option.

If you have not finished the real test after 45 minutes has elapsed, you will not be allowed to complete it. The CD-ROM practice tests replicate this insofar as you will be informed of the moment you run out of time.

❝ The CD-ROM that accompanies this book is designed to help you learn and revise the official Home Office study material. Although similar to the actual test you will need to take, there are also some significant differences. ❞

Preparing for the test

You can sit and resit the Life in the UK Test as many times as you want. However, every time you take it, you will need to pay an administration fee. It makes financial sense, therefore, to do what you can to ensure that you pass first time. In addition to learning the material you will be tested on, it is a good idea to familiarise yourself with the test process. This will help you be as prepared as possible.

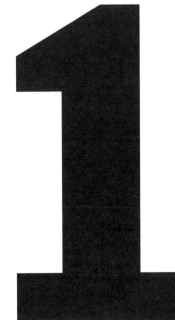

About the test

The most important part of your preparation for the Life in the UK Test is to read and learn the information contained in Chapters 2-6. However, it is also a good idea to familiarise yourself with the format and process of the test itself.

You will be given 45 minutes to complete the Life in the UK Test. In order to pass, you will need to answer 75% of the questions correctly. This equates to about 18 of the 24 questions in total. You will be told shortly after the test, while you are still at the test centre, whether you have passed the test or not. If you have passed, you will be given a notification letter confirming so. When you submit your application for citizenship or for indefinite leave to remain, you will need to submit this notification letter as part of the documentation in support of your application. In addition, the test centre will inform the UK Border Agency of your pass. This can take up to a week, so if you plan to submit your citizenship application in person, it is a good idea to wait for at least a week after the test before you do so.

❝ The test centre will inform the UK Border Agency when you pass the test. This can take up to a week, so if you plan to submit your citizenship application in person, it is a good idea to wait for at least a week after the test before you do so. ❞

There are about 100 test centres located throughout the United Kingdom, the Isle of Man and the Channel Islands. With the exception of the Isle of Man and the Channel Islands, you will need to take the test on a computer located at one of the test centres. Tests taken in the Channel Islands and Isle of Man

 Your pass notification letter is very important: you should keep it in a safe place until you are ready to fill in your citizenship application. If you lose this letter, you will not be given a new one to replace it. The letter does not have an expiry date.

are paper-based. They include 25 questions, as opposed to 24, six of which will be based on local information specific to the island where you are taking the test. If you want to take the test in one of the Channel Islands or the Isle of Man, you will need to contact the Immigration and Nationality Service department of that island's governing body. This department will provide you with information on the location of the test centre (for example, in Guernsey, this is in the College of Further Education). The department will also provide you with a supplementary booklet outlining the information and history of the island that you will need to know in order to answer six of the test questions. You will need to learn this booklet in addition to the official study material outlined in Chapters 2 to 6 of this book. For the contact information of each of these islands' immigration departments, see Useful addresses on page 206. If you are sitting the test in England, Northern Ireland, Scotland or Wales, you can expect some of the questions to relate to the region in which you are taking the test. These are all taken from the official study material and you will not need a supplementary booklet to answer them.

TAKING THE TEST

Once you feel confident that you have learnt the material contained here, in Chapters 2-6, and you are happy with the level of your computer skills, your first step should be to find and register with a test centre. To find a test centre near you, use the 'find a test centre' tool on the Life in the UK Test website, www.lifeintheuktest.gov.uk. After submitting your postcode the tool will provide you with a list of centres close to where you live, along with the distance in miles and a location map of each centre. Alternatively you may call the Life in the UK Test helpline on 0800 015 4245. There is also a choice of helplines offered in other languages. These are listed on page 10.

Booking a test

You may book a test directly with a test centre, either in person or by telephone. The centre should be able to offer you a test date between one and four weeks from the date that you contact them. Different centres offer differing testing days. If the first centre you contact cannot offer you your preferred date, you should try another test centre.

Test fees

You will need to pay an administrative fee of £34 to take the Life in the UK Test. However, this figure is currently under review as HM Revenue and

Customs have ruled that the test fees should be subject to VAT. If you need to cancel or postpone your test, some test centres additionally charge a cancellation fee, typically of about £10, to cover any administrative costs. You should check the cancellation policy of your test centre for confirmation of this.

Each test centre has its own preferred payment methods. However, most request payment in advance by cash or cheque. Some also accept credit and debit cards.

Test administration

On arrival for your test you will need to prove who you are through photographic identification. You will need to show one of the following forms of ID to the test supervisor:

- Your passport
- A UK photocard driving licence
- A Home Office Convention Travel Document (CTD)
- A Home Office Certificate of Identity Document (CID)
- A Home Office Stateless Person Document (SPD)
- An Immigration Status Document, endorsed with a UK Residence Permit and carrying your photograph.

You will also be asked for confirmation of your current UK address. You may do this by showing your UK driving licence, or a document such as a utility bill or bank statement.

If you have already been in contact with the Home Office regarding your citizenship application, you will have been given a reference number. It is useful if you can bring this with you to the test centre as it will assist the administration process.

Accommodating individual needs

Most test centres have wheelchair access and toilets. To confirm what facilities are available in your local test centre, you can check the notes on the centre's webpage (it will be contained within the results of the 'find a test centre' tool) on the Life in the UK Test website. Alternatively, you may ring and ask direct.

If you have a visual impairment, it is possible to select a larger font size, high contrast or high visibility for the test. Large font comprises a larger type size placed on the standard test background. High contrast uses large black lettering placed against a cream-coloured background. High visibility employs a large yellow font against a black background.

If you prefer, the computer can read out each question for you. In some cases it is also possible for someone to help you enter your answer on the computer. You may also obtain an audio CD version of the Home Office study material, *Life in the United Kingdom: A Journey to Citizenship*.

To discuss how these or any other individual need may be accommodated by the test centre, you should contact the test supervisor at your local centre direct when you first book a test date.

Language

You will normally have to take the test in English. Your level of English comprehension will need to be high enough to succeed. This means that you should be able to achieve what is referred to as English for Speakers of Other Languages (ESOL) Level 3 or above. If you are sitting the test in Wales or Scotland, you may also choose to take the test in Welsh or Scottish Gaelic respectively. You can contact your local test centre for further details.

FAILING THE TEST

If you cannot answer 18 or more of the questions correctly, you will fail the test. Don't worry if you do, however, for you can simply retake it when you feel ready (although the earliest you can do so is seven days later). Your results notification letter will give you feedback on which areas of *Life in the United Kingdom: A Journey to Citizenship* you need to look at again. You will then need to book a new test date and time with your test centre.

You can retake the test as many times as you need to. However, you will not be able to make an application for indefinite leave to remain or citizenship if you cannot pass the test, or the ESOL and citizenship courses.

Study tip: If you fail the test

If you fail your test, it is a good idea to avoid booking up another test as soon as possible. Try to give yourself enough time to go back to the study text and revise. Look at which areas you were particularly weak on and give them some extra focus.

Computer skills

You will need basic computer skills, including competence with a keyboard and mouse, to take the Life in the UK Test. This section provides an overview of the type of skills you will need for certain tasks.

The test centres in England, Northern Ireland, Scotland and Wales will only offer the Life in the UK Test on a computer. There are no other versions of the test.

Don't worry if you have never used a computer before. The test is designed to be easy to use and test supervisors specialise in providing support for people who are less confident about using a computer. You can also get help and advice on how to use one at your local UK Online Centre. There are more than 6,000 centres around the country in a variety of locations including libraries, internet cafes and community centres. At a UK Online Centre you can practise using a computer for free or a very low cost. If there is not a UK Online Centre close to where you live, contact your local library. Most libraries can provide access to computers and advice on how to use them for free, or for a low cost.

The Life in the UK Test website, www.lifeintheuktest.gov.uk contains a section designed to help you navigate the computer. Mouse training includes a mini-tutorial on basic mouse skills and shows you how to select and deselect answers on your test. The section on keyboard training illustrates what type of keyboard you will need to use in the test, as well as the keys you can use to move around the test itself. A navigational tutorial also shows how to move around the test, and gives examples of the types of questions used in the test.

In addition to practising your computer skills on the Life in the UK Test website, you will be given the opportunity to complete a practice test at

 To find a UK Online Centre near you, call 0800 77 1234 or use the search facility on their website at www.ukonlinecentres.com

your test centre before you begin your test. This will appear as a choice you can opt for after you have been logged-on and set up on your test computer. It is a good idea to take the practice test and is recommended by the Home Office Border and Immigration Agency.

❝ Don't worry if you have never used a computer before. The test is designed to be easy to use and test supervisors specialise in providing support. ❞

USING THE CD-ROM

The practice tests included on the CD-ROM that accompany this book are designed to reflect the style and approach of the actual Home Office Life in the UK Test.

What to look out for on the test screen

At the top of every test screen you will see a **clock**. This counts down the time from when you start the test. Halfway through the allocated test time of 45 minutes, you will get a time alert. You will get two more time alerts 10 and 2 minutes before the test ends.

Each of the **24 boxes** along the top of the screen represents a question. You can move to any question by simply clicking on a box with your mouse or a keyboard shortcut (see page 24).

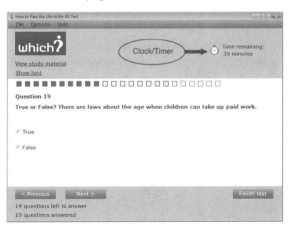

Clock / Timer

A **box** with a **thin outline** means that you have not answered a question. A **box** with a **bold outline** means that you have visited the question but not answered it. A **solid box** means that you have answered the question.

You can also move to another question by clicking on **Next** at the bottom of the screen.

Answered and unanswered questions

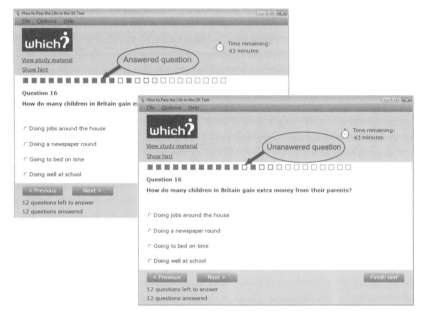

What types of questions will I have to answer?

There are four types of questions you will have to answer:

1 Asks for one correct answer out of four possible answers.
2 Asks you to decide whether a statement is **TRUE** or **FALSE**.
3 Asks you to select **TWO** correct answers from four possible answers.
4 Asks you to select which one of **TWO** statements is correct.

How do I select an answer?

When you move your cursor – that is, the arrow symbol that you can move around the screen by moving your mouse – to an answer the entire line the answer appears on will turn grey. This means that it is ready for you to select it. If you are using a mouse, the arrow-pointer will change to the image of a hand with a pointing finger. Once you click on a circle/square button to select an answer, the area around it will turn light blue and a dot will appear next to the answer you have picked. Click on **Next** at the bottom of the screen or the next box at the top of the screen to view the next question.

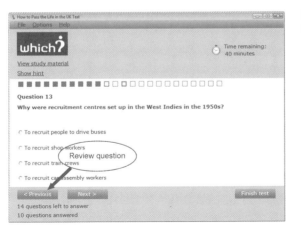

Selecting answers

How do I review a question?

Clicking on a box at the top of the screen lets you visit a question first and then return to answer it later. This is really useful when you aren't sure what the answer is. Once you have answered a question, you can review it by clicking on **Previous** at the bottom of the screen.

Reviewing questions

What do I do if I can't answer a question?

If you can't answer a question on the accompanying CD-ROM, click on **Show hint** at the top of the screen. The area around the correct answer will flash light blue.

Show hint

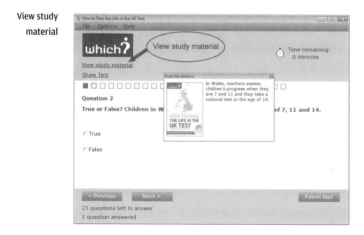

You can also access the official study material related to a particular question by clicking on **View study material** at the top of the screen.

View study material

What happens once I have finished the test?

Clicking on the **Finish test** button at the bottom of the screen ends the test.

Don't worry if you select **Finish test** by mistake, you will be asked to confirm your decision. Remember: none of your answers are final until you select **Finish test** and confirm your decision.

Once you have done this, a summary of your test results will appear detailing the time you took, how many questions you answered, your score and the percentage of correct answers. To review the correct answers, click on **Next** and then **Previous**.

Test summary

What do I do if I run out of time?

If you run out of time, your test will end automatically and you will not be allowed to finish your current question.

Timeout alert

Can I use keyboard shortcuts?

When taking the test you can use keyboard shortcuts or a mouse.
The shortcuts for answering questions are as follows:

To select the **first answer** press **1**.
To select the **second answer** press **2**.
To select the **third answer** press **3**.
To select the **fourth answer** press **4**.
To deselect an answer, press the relevant number key again.

Answer
shortcuts

Other shortcuts:
To move to the next question, press the letter **N**.
To move to the previous question, press the letter **P**.
To finish the test, press the letter **F**.

Shortcut
keys

A changing society

From the key reasons for immigration to the UK, to the proportion of young people going onto higher education, this chapter explores key aspects of Britain's society. Learn more about the way society has changed, particularly in terms of equal rights for women. In addition, find out about the educational opportunities available for children and young people.

Migration to Britain

This section looks at patterns of migration to the UK over history and suggests reasons why migrants wanted to settle here. It also refers to changes in the UK's immigration laws.

In this section there is information about:
- The long history of immigration to the United Kingdom
- Different reasons why people migrated to the UK
- Basic changes in immigration patterns over the last 30 years.

Many people living in Britain today have their origins in other countries. They can trace their roots to regions throughout the world such as Europe, the Middle East, Africa, Asia and the Caribbean. In the distant past, invaders came to Britain, seized land and stayed. More recently, people come to Britain to find safety, jobs and a better life.

Britain is proud of its tradition of offering safety to people who are escaping persecution and hardship. For example, in the 16th and 18th centuries, Huguenots (French Protestants) came to Britain to escape religious persecution in France. In the mid–1840s there was a terrible famine in Ireland and many Irish people migrated to Britain. Many Irish men became labourers and helped to build canals and railways across Britain.

From 1880 to 1910, a large number of Jewish people came to Britain to escape racist attacks (called 'pogroms') in what was then called the Russian Empire and from the countries now called Poland, Ukraine and Belarus.

❝ Britain is proud of its tradition of offering safety to people who are escaping persecution and hardship. ❞

MIGRATION SINCE 1945

After the Second World War (1939–45), there was a huge task of rebuilding Britain. There were not enough people to do the work, so the British government encouraged workers from Ireland and other parts of

Study tip: Give yourself time

Don't try and cram the information contained in the book *Life in the United Kingdom: A Journey to Citizenship* the night before the test. Give yourself as much time as you can to learn the information. Draw up a revision timetable. This will help you plan your learning and will make you feel in control and calm. Be realistic, however, and don't forget to give yourself some time off to relax.

Europe to come to the UK to help with the reconstruction. In 1948, people from the West Indies were also invited to come and work.

During the 1950s, there was still a shortage of labour in the UK. The UK encouraged immigration in the 1950s for economic reasons and many industries advertised for workers from overseas. For example, centres were set up in the West Indies to recruit people to drive buses. Textile and engineering firms from the north of England and the Midlands sent agents to India and Pakistan to find workers. For about 25 years, people from the West Indies, India, Pakistan, and later Bangladesh, travelled to work and settle in Britain.

The number of people migrating from these areas fell in the late 1960s and early 1970s because the Government passed new laws to restrict immigration to Britain, although immigrants from 'old' Commonwealth countries such as Australia, New Zealand and Canada did not have to face such strict controls. During this time, however, the UK was able to help a large number of refugees. In 1972 the UK accepted thousands of people of Indian origin who had been forced to leave Uganda. Another programme to help people from Vietnam was introduced in the late 1970s. Since 1979, more than 25,000 refugees from South East Asia have been allowed to settle in the UK.

In the 1980s the largest immigrant groups came from the United States, Australia, South Africa, and New Zealand. In the early 1990s, groups of people from the former Soviet Union came to Britain looking for a new and safer way of life. Since 1994 there has been a global rise in mass migration for both political and economic reasons.

Check that you understand
- Some of the historical reasons for immigration to the UK
- Some of the reasons for immigration to the UK since 1945
- The main immigrant groups coming to the UK since 1945, the countries they came from and kind of work they did

The changing role of women

This area reflects how society's attitudes towards women have changed over time. It includes information on women's rights and discrimination in the workplace, as well as examining how employment and education opportunities for women have altered.

In this section there is information about:
- Changes to family structures and women's rights since the 19th century
- Women's campaigns for rights, including the right to vote in the late 19th and early 20th centuries
- Discrimination against women in the workplace and in education
- Changing attitudes to women working, and responsibilities of men and women in the home

In 19th century Britain, families were usually large and in many poorer homes men, women and children all contributed towards the family income. Although they made an important economic contribution, women in Britain had fewer rights than men. Until 1857, a married woman had no right to divorce her husband. Until 1882, when a woman got married, her earnings, property and money automatically belonged to her husband.

In the late 19th and early 20th centuries, an increasing number of women campaigned and demonstrated for greater rights and, in particular, the right to vote. They became known as 'Suffragettes'. These protests decreased during the First World War because women joined in the war effort and therefore did a much greater variety of work than they had before. When the First World War ended in 1918, women over the age of 30 were finally given the right to vote and to stand for election to

 For further information on discrimination in the workplace, see Chapter 6.

Parliament. It was not until 1928 that women won the right to vote at 21, at the same age as men.

Despite these improvements, women still faced discrimination in the workplace. For example, it was quite common for employers to ask women to leave their jobs when they got married. Many jobs were closed to women and it was difficult for women to enter universities. During the 1960s and 1970s there was increasing pressure from women for equal rights. Parliament passed new laws giving women the right to equal pay and prohibiting employers from discriminating against women because of their sex (see also Chapter 6).

WOMEN IN BRITAIN TODAY

Women in Britain today make up 51% of the population and 45% of the workforce. These days girls leave school, on average, with better qualifications than boys and there are now more women than men at university.

Employment opportunities for women are now much greater than they were in the past. Although women continue to be employed in traditional female areas such as healthcare, teaching, secretarial and retail work, there is strong evidence that attitudes are changing, and women are now active in a much wider range of work than before. Research shows that very few people today believe that women in Britain should stay at home and not go out to work. Today, almost three-quarters of women with school-age children are in paid work.

In most households, women continue to have the main responsibility for childcare and housework. There is evidence that there is now greater equality in homes and that more men are taking some responsibility for raising the family and doing housework. Despite this progress, many people believe that more needs to be done to achieve greater equality for women. There are still examples of discrimination against women, particularly in the workplace, despite the laws that exist to prevent it. Women still do not always have the same access to promotion and better-paid jobs. The average hourly pay rate for women is 20% less than for men, and after leaving university most women still earn less than men.

Check that you understand
- When women aged over 30 were first given the right to vote
- When women were given equal voting rights with men
- Some of the important developments to create equal rights in the workplace

Children, family and young people

The section explores patterns of family life. It looks at education and areas that may affect young people, including tobacco, alcohol and drugs. It also examines the relationship many young people have with politics.

In this section there is information about:
- The identity, interests, tastes and lifestyle patterns of children and young people
- Education and work
- Health hazards: cigarettes, alcohol and illegal drugs
- Young people's political and social attitudes

In the UK, there are almost 15 million children and young people up to the age of 19. This is almost one–quarter of the UK population.

Over the last 20 years, family patterns in Britain have been transformed because of changing attitudes towards divorce and separation. Today, 65% of children live with both birth parents, almost 25% live in lone–parent families, and 10% live within a stepfamily. Most children in Britain receive weekly pocket money from their parents and many get extra money for doing jobs around the house.

❝Over the last 20 years, family patterns in Britain have been transformed because of changing attitudes towards divorce and separation.❞

Children in the UK do not play outside the home as much as they did in the past. Part of the reason for this is increased home entertainment such as television, videos and computers. There is also increased concern for children's safety and there are many stories in newspapers about child molestation by strangers, but there is no evidence that this kind of danger is increasing.

Study tip: Read the chapters

If you confine your learning to the practice test questions and answers in this book and CD, you may put yourself at a disadvantage. The Home Office Border and Immigration Agency guards the secrecy of the actual exam questions very closely. The questions contained in this study guide are designed to help you learn by closely replicating the style of the real questions. To give yourself the best chance, however, you should study the text contained within Chapters 2 to 6 and use the practice questions as prompts.

Young people have different identities, interests and fashions to older people. Many young people move away from their family home when they become adults but this varies from one community to another.

EDUCATION

The law states that children between the ages of 5 and 16 must attend school. The tests that pupils take are very important, and in England and Scotland children take national tests in English, mathematics and science when they are 7, 11 and 14 years old. (In Wales, teachers assess children's progress when they are 7 and 11 and they take a national test at the age of 14). The tests give important information about children's progress and achievement, the subjects they are doing well in and the areas where they need extra help.

Most young people take the General Certificate of Secondary Education (GCSE), or, in Scotland, Scottish Qualifications Authority (SQA) Standard Grade examinations when they are 16. At 17 and 18, many take vocational qualifications, General Certificates of Education at an Advanced level (AGCEs), AS level units or Higher/Advanced Higher Grades in Scotland. Schools and colleges will expect good GCSE or SQA Standard Grade results before allowing a student to enrol on an AGCE or Scottish Higher/Advanced Higher course.

 In October 2008, the Government abolished mandatory Key Stage tests (SATs) for children aged 14. However, for the purposes of the current Life in the UK Test, which is based on the official text reproduced here, children sit SATs tests at ages 7, 11 and 14.

AS levels are Advanced Subsidiary qualifications gained by completing three AS units. Three AS units are considered as one–half of an AGCE. In the second part of the course, three more AS units can be studied to complete the AGCE qualification.

Many people refer to AGCEs by the old name of A levels. AGCEs are the traditional route for entry to higher education courses, but many higher education students enter with different kinds of qualifications.

One in three young people now go on to higher education at college or university. Some young people defer their university entrance for a year and take a 'gap year'. This year out of education often includes voluntary work and travel overseas. Some young people work to earn and save money to pay for their university fees and living expenses.

People over 16 years of age may also choose to study at Colleges of Further Education or Adult Education Centres. There is a wide range of academic and vocational courses available as well as courses which develop leisure interests and skills. Contact your local college for details.

WORK

It is common for young people to have a part-time job while they are still at school. It is thought there are 2 million children at work at any one time. The most common jobs are newspaper delivery and work in supermarkets and newsagents. Many parents believe that part-time work helps children to become more independent as well as providing them (and sometimes their families) with extra income.

 For further information on children's work rights, see www.worksmart.org.uk

There are laws about the age when children can take up paid work (usually not before 14), the type of work they can do and the number of hours they can work (see www.worksmart.org.uk for more information).

It is very important to note that there are concerns for the safety of children who work illegally or who are not properly supervised and the employment of children is strictly controlled by law.

HEALTH HAZARDS

Many parents worry that their children may misuse drugs and addictive substances.

Smoking

Although cigarette smoking is slowly falling in the adult population, more young people are smoking, and more school age girls smoke than boys. From 1 October 2007 it is illegal to sell tobacco products to anyone under 18 years old. Smoking is generally not allowed in public buildings and work places throughout the UK.

Alcohol

Young people under the age of 18 are not allowed to buy alcohol in Britain, but there is concern about the age some young people start drinking alcohol and the amount of alcohol they drink at one time, known as 'binge drinking'. It is illegal to be drunk in public and there are now more penalties to help control this problem, including on-the-spot fines.

Check that you understand
- The proportion of all young people who go on to higher education
- Lifestyle patterns of children and young people (e.g. pocket money, leaving home on reaching adulthood)
- Changing family patterns and attitudes to changing family patterns (e.g. divorce)
- That education in Britain is free and compulsory, and that there is compulsory testing (in England and Scotland) at ages 7, 11 and 14; there are also GCSE and/or vocational exams at 16; and Advanced level exams (A and AS) at ages 17 and 18
- That there is a government target that half of all young people attend higher education
- That there are strict laws regarding the employment of children
- That there are important health concerns and laws relating to children and young people and smoking, alcohol and drugs
- That young people are eligible to vote in elections from age 18

Illegal drugs

As in most countries, it is illegal to possess drugs such as heroin, cocaine, ecstasy, amphetamines and cannabis. Current statistics show that half of all young adults, and about a third of the population as a whole, have used illegal drugs at one time or another.

There is a strong link between the use of hard drugs (e.g. crack cocaine and heroin) and crime, and also hard drugs and mental illness. The misuse of drugs has a huge social and financial cost for the country. This is a serious issue and British society needs to find an effective way of dealing with the problem.

YOUNG PEOPLE'S POLITICAL AND SOCIAL ATTITUDES

Young people in Britain can vote in elections from the age of 18. In the 2001 general election, however, only 1 in 5 first-time voters used their vote. There has been a great debate over the reasons for this. Some researchers think that one reason is that young people are not interested in the political process.

Although most young people show little interest in party politics, there is strong evidence that many are interested in specific political issues such as the environment and cruelty to animals.

In 2003 a survey of young people in England and Wales showed that they believe the five most important issues in Britain were crime, drugs, war/terrorism, racism and health. The same survey asked young people about their participation in political and community events. They found that 86% of young people had taken part in some form of community event over the past year, and 50% had taken part in fund-raising or collecting money for charity. Similar results have been found in surveys in Scotland and Northern Ireland. Many children first get involved in these activities while at school where they study Citizenship as part of the National Curriculum.

Check that you understand the key terms and vocabulary for this chapter

Migration to Britain:
- Migrate, immigrate, immigration, immigrant
- Persecution, famine, conflict
- Labour, labourer
- Recruit
- Restrict
- Political asylum
- The war effort

Changing role of women:
- Income, earnings
- Rights, equal rights
- Campaign, demonstrate
- Discriminate, discrimination
- Prohibit
- Workforce
- Household
- Promotion

Children, family and young people:
- Eligible
- Concern
- Molestation
- Attitudes
- Hazards

- Birth parent, stepfamily
- Compulsory
- Informal
- Methods of assessment
- Defer
- Gap year
- Independent
- Income
- Misuse
- Addictive substances
- Abuse
- Binge drinking
- On-the-spot fines
- Controlled drugs
- Criminal offence
- Possess
- Heroin, cocaine, crack cocaine, ecstasy, amphetamines, cannabis
- Burglary, mugging
- Debate
- Politicians, political process, party politics, political issues
- Specific
- Concern
- Environment
- Terrorism, racism
- Participation
- Fund-raising

For further information on the meanings of words and phrases used in this book, see the Glossary on pages 200–205.

A changing society

Practice questions

For the answers to these questions, see page 190.

1 **True or False? Britain is proud of its tradition of offering safety to people who are escaping persecution and hardship.**
A True
B False

2 **Who were the Huguenots?**
A French Protestants
B French Catholics
C French Jews
D French Hindus

3 **Why did a large number of Jewish people come to Britain between 1880 and 1910?**
A To escape racist attacks
B To set up businesses
C To escape economic hardship
D To escape famine

4 **What exams do many young people in England and Wales take at the age of 17 or 18?**
A AGCEs and AS levels
B Higher/Advanced Higher Grades
C Scottish Extended Levels
D SQAA (Scottish Qualifications Advanced Authority)

5 **Why did the British Government encourage the immigration of workers after the Second World War?**
A To replace people killed in the war
B To help with the task of rebuilding Britain
C To help people escape communism
D To help people escape poverty

6 **What TWO sorts of work did the Irish men who came to Britain in the mid-1840s largely do? (Select two options)**
A They weaved cloth
B They farmed the land
C They built canals
D They built railways

7 **What is the Government's target for young people to attend higher education?**
A That all young people will attend higher education
B That most young people will attend higher education
C That half of all young people will attend higher education
D That a quarter of all young people will attend higher education

8 When did the First World War end?

A 1914

B 1916

C 1918

D 1920

9 Why did migration from the West Indies, India, Pakistan and Bangladesh fall in the late 1960s?

A The government passed new laws to restrict immigration to Britain

B There were no more job vacancies in Britain

C These countries prevented their workers leaving

D There was a housing shortage in Britain

10 From which two countries did a large number of refugees come to the UK during the 1970s? (Select two options)

A India

B Vietnam

C The Soviet Union

D Uganda

11 What did many industries do during the 1950s to attract workers from overseas?

A Advertised for workers

B Offered free housing in Britain

C Paid higher salaries

D Arranged free flights for interested workers and their families

12 In 2003, what percentage of young people were reported to have taken part in some form of community event over the previous year?

A 56%

B 66%

C 76%

D 86%

13 True or False? Women in the UK today have to stop work when they get married?

A True

B False

14 What is the minimum age that you can buy alcohol in Britain?

A 14

B 16

C 18

D 21

15 True or False? In 19th-century Britain, men had greater rights than women.

A True

B False

16 What percentage of children live within a stepfamily?

A 10%

B 15%

C 20%

D 25%

17 True or False? Generally, smoking in public buildings is not allowed.

A True

B False

18 From what age can people in the UK vote?

A 16

B 18

C 21

D 30

19 True or False? Citizenship is studied by many children in Britain as part of the National Curriculum.

A True

B False

20 During what period did an increasing number of women hold demonstrations and campaign for greater rights and the right to vote?

A In the late 16th century and early 17th century

B In the late 17th century and early 18th century

C In the late 18th century and early 19th century

D In the late 19th century and early 20th century

21 What were women who campaigned and demonstrated for greater rights called?

A Sufferers

B Suffragettes

C Liberators

D Freedom fighters

22 How long did the Second World War last?

A 4 years

B 6 years

C 7 years

D 8 years

23 How many children and young people up to the age of 19 are there in the UK?

A Almost 10 million

B Almost 15 million

C Almost 20 million

D Almost 25 million

24 Which of these statements is correct?

A During the 1960s and 1970s Parliament passed new laws giving women equal pay

B During the 1980s and 1990s Parliament passed new laws giving women equal pay

25 True or False? Family patterns in Britain have been transformed because of changing attitudes towards divorce and separation.

A True

B False

26 In the 2001 general election, what percentage of potential first-time voters used their vote?

A 20%

B 40%

C 60%

D 80%

27 True or False? Education for children between the ages of 5 and 16 in Britain is compulsory.

A True

B False

28 When were immigrants from the West Indies first actively invited to come to the United Kingdom?

A 1928

B 1938

C 1948

D 1958

29 True or False? There is strong evidence that attitudes are changing, and women are now active in a much wider range of work than before.

A True

B False

30 True or False? There are laws governing the age when children can take up paid work.

A True

B False

UK today: a profile

Thanks largely to immigration, the population of the UK today is growing. Although the majority of the population is white British, the country is ethnically diverse. This chapter explores how information on the population is gathered through the census. It also looks at the UK's regional differences and national customs, including religion, traditions and festivals.

Population

The UK's ethnically diverse population is growing faster today than ever before. This is thanks in large part to the influx of people arriving from overseas. Such information is gathered and recorded every ten years in the UK's census.

In this section there is information about:
- The population of the UK
- The census
- Ethnic diversity

In 2005 the population of the United Kingdom was just under 60 million people.

UK population 2005	UK population %	million
England	(84% of the population)	50.1
Scotland	(8% of the population)	5.1
Wales	(5% of the population)	2.9
Northern Ireland	(3% of the population)	1.7
Total UK		59.8

Source: National Statistics

The population has grown by 7.7% since 1971, and growth has been faster in more recent years. Although the general population in the UK has increased in the last 20 years, in some areas such as the North-East and North-West of England there has been a decline.

Both the birth rate and the death rate are falling and as a result the UK now has an ageing population. For instance, there are more people over 60 than children under 16. There is also a record number of people aged 85 and over.

THE CENSUS

A census is a count of the whole population. It also collects statistics on topics such as age, place of birth, occupation, ethnicity, housing, health, and marital status.

A census has been taken every ten years since 1801, except during the Second World War. The next census will take place in 2011.

During a census, a form is delivered to every household in the country. This form asks for detailed information about each member of the household and must be completed by law. The information remains confidential and anonymous; it can only be released to the public after 100 years, when many people researching their family history find it very useful. General census information is used to identify population trends and to help planning. More information about the census, the census form and statistics from previous censuses can be found at www.statistics.gov.uk/census

ETHNIC DIVERSITY

The UK population is ethnically diverse and is changing rapidly, especially in large cities such as London, so it is not always easy to get an exact picture of the ethnic origin of all the population from census statistics. Each of the four countries of the UK (England, Wales, Scotland and Northern Ireland) has different customs, attitudes and histories.

People of Indian, Pakistani, Chinese, Black Caribbean, Black African, Bangladeshi and mixed ethnic descent make up 8.3% of the UK population. Today about half the members of these communities were born in the United Kingdom.

There are also considerable numbers of people resident in the UK who are of Irish, Italian, Greek and Turkish Cypriot, Polish, Australian, Canadian, New Zealand and American descent. Large numbers have also arrived since 2004 from the new East European member states of the European Union. These groups are not identified separately in the census statistics in the following table.

For more information about the census, the census form and statistics from previous censuses see, www.statistics.gov.uk/census

UK population 2001	million	UK population %
White (including people of European, Australian, American descent)	54.2	92.0
Mixed	0.7	1.2
Asian or Asian British		
Indian	1.1	1.8
Pakistani	0.7	1.3
Bangladeshi	0.3	0.5
Other Asian	0.2	0.4
Black or Black British		
Black Caribbean	0.6	1.0
Black African	0.5	0.8
Black other	0.1	0.2
Chinese	0.2	0.4
Other	0.2	0.4

Source: National Statistics from the 2001 census

WHERE DO THE LARGEST ETHNIC MINORITY GROUPS LIVE?

The figures from the 2001 census show that most members of the large ethnic minority groups in the UK live in England, where they make up 9% of the total population. 45% of all ethnic minority people live in the London area, where they form nearly one-third of the population (29%). Other areas of England with large ethnic minority populations are the West Midlands, the South East, the North West, and Yorkshire and Humberside.

Proportion of ethnic minority groups in the countries of the UK			
England	9%	Scotland	2%
Wales	2%	Northern Ireland	less than 1%

Check that you understand
- The size of the current UK population
- The population of Scotland, Wales and Northern Ireland
- What the census is and when the next one will be
- What the largest ethnic minorities in the UK are
- Where most ethnic minority people live

The nations and regions of the UK

This section discusses cultural differences between the UK's four major regions: England, Scotland, Northern Ireland and Wales. This includes the languages and dialects spoken in the different regions.

In this section there is information about:
- The regions of Britain

The UK is a medium-sized country. The longest distance on the mainland, from John O'Groats on the north coast of Scotland to Land's End in the south-west corner of England, is about 870 miles (approximately 1,400 kilometres). Most of the population live in towns and cities.

There are many variations in culture and language in the different parts of the United Kingdom. This is seen in differences in architecture, in some local customs, in types of food, and especially in language. The English language has many accents and dialects. These are a clear indication of regional differences in the UK. Well-known dialects in England are Geordie (Tyneside), Scouse (Liverpool) and Cockney (London). Many other languages in addition to English are spoken in the UK, especially in multicultural cities.

In Wales, Scotland and Northern Ireland, people speak different varieties and dialects of English. In Wales, too, an increasing number of people speak Welsh, which is taught in schools and universities. In Scotland Gaelic is spoken in some parts of the Highlands and Islands and in Northern Ireland a few people speak Irish Gaelic. Some of the dialects of English spoken in Scotland show the influence of the old Scottish language, Scots. One of the dialects spoken in Northern Ireland is called Ulster Scots.

Check that you understand
- What languages other than English are spoken in Wales, Scotland and Northern Ireland
- Some of the ways you can identify regional differences in the UK

Religion

This section identifies the major religious beliefs held by people in the UK. It recognises the historically Christian nature of the UK's society and how only a minority of people actually attend religious services.

In this section there is information about:
- Religion and religious freedom

Although the UK is historically a Christian society, everyone has the legal right to practise the religion of their choice. In the 2001 census, just over 75% said they had a religion: 7 out of 10 of these were Christians. There were also a considerable number of people who followed other religions. Although many people in the UK said they held religious beliefs, currently only around 10% of the population attend religious services. More people attend services in Scotland and Northern Ireland than in England and Wales. In London the number of people who attend religious services is increasing.

&& Although the UK is historically a Christian society, everyone has the legal right to practise the religion of their choice. ,,

Religions in the UK	%
Christian (10% of whom are Roman Catholic)	71.6
Muslim	2.7
Hindu	1.0
Sikh	0.6
Jewish	0.5
Buddhist	0.3
Other	0.3
Total All	77.0
No religion	15.5
Not stated	7.3

Source: National Statistics from the 2001 census

Study tip: Think positive

Many psychologists believe that you can make yourself feel more positive by visualising your test going well. To do this, imagine you are confident and relaxed during the test. Try to imagine the scene in as much detail as possible. Go back and revisualise this as often as you can in the days leading up to your test.

THE CHRISTIAN CHURCHES

In England there is a constitutional link between church and state. The official church of the state is the Church of England. The Church of England is called the Anglican Church in other countries and the Episcopal Church in Scotland and in the USA. The Church of England is a Protestant church and has existed since the Reformation in the 1530s. The king or queen (the monarch) is the head, or Supreme Governor, of the Church of England. The monarch is not allowed to marry anyone who is not Protestant.

The spiritual leader of the Church of England is the Archbishop of Canterbury. The monarch has the right to select the Archbishop and other senior church officials, but usually the choice is made by the Prime Minister and a committee appointed by the Church. Several Church of England bishops sit in the House of Lords (see chapter 4). The Church of Scotland is Presbyterian, national and free from state control. It has no bishops and is governed for spiritual purposes by a series of courts, so its most senior representative is the Moderator (chairperson). There is no established church in Wales or in Northern Ireland.

❝ The official church of the state is the Church of England. The Church of England is called the Anglican Church in other countries and the Episcopal Church in Scotland and in the USA. ❞

Other Protestant Christian groups in the UK are Baptists, Presbyterians, Methodists and Quakers. 10% of Christians are Roman Catholic (40% in Northern Ireland).

PATRON SAINTS

England, Scotland, Wales and Northern Ireland each have a national saint called a patron saint. Each saint has a feast day. In the past these were celebrated as holy days when many people had a day off work. Today these are not public holidays except for 17 March in Northern Ireland.

Patron saints' days

St David's Day, Wales	1 March
St Patrick's Day, Northern Ireland	17 March
St George's Day, England	23 April
St Andrew's Day, Scotland	30 November

There are four 'Bank Holidays' and four other public holidays a year (most people call all these holidays Bank Holidays).

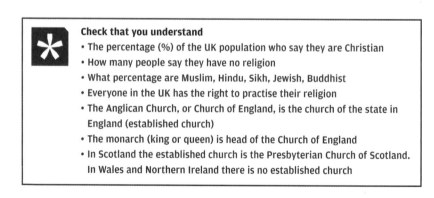

Check that you understand
- The percentage (%) of the UK population who say they are Christian
- How many people say they have no religion
- What percentage are Muslim, Hindu, Sikh, Jewish, Buddhist
- Everyone in the UK has the right to practise their religion
- The Anglican Church, or Church of England, is the church of the state in England (established church)
- The monarch (king or queen) is head of the Church of England
- In Scotland the established church is the Presbyterian Church of Scotland. In Wales and Northern Ireland there is no established church

Customs and traditions

This section provides an overview of the UK's major customs and traditions. It includes festivals and important dates throughout the calendar, from the Edinburgh Festival to Christmas Day and the FA Cup Final.

In this section there is information about:
• Customs and traditions

FESTIVALS

Throughout the year there are festivals of art, music and culture, such as the Notting Hill Carnival in west London and the Edinburgh Festival. Customs and traditions from various religions, such as Eid ul-Fitr (Muslim), Diwali (Hindu) and Hanukkah (Jewish) are widely recognised in the UK. Children learn about these at school. The main Christian festivals are Christmas and Easter. There are also celebrations of non-religious traditions such as New Year.

THE MAIN CHRISTIAN FESTIVALS

Christmas Day

25 December, celebrates the birth of Jesus Christ. It is a public holiday. Many Christians go to church on Christmas Eve (24 December) or on Christmas Day itself. Christmas is also usually celebrated by people who are not Christian. People usually spend the day at home and eat a special meal, which often includes turkey. They give each other gifts, send each other cards and decorate their houses. Many people decorate a tree. Christmas is a special time for children. Very young children believe that an old man, Father Christmas (or Santa Claus), brings them presents during the night. He is always shown in pictures with a long white beard, dressed in red. Boxing Day, 26 December, is the day after Christmas. It is a public holiday.

OTHER FESTIVALS AND TRADITIONS

New Year

1 January, is a public holiday. People usually celebrate on the night of 31 December. In Scotland, 31 December is called Hogmanay and 2 January is also a public holiday. In Scotland, Hogmanay is a bigger holiday for some people than Christmas.

Valentine's Day

14 February, is when lovers exchange cards and gifts. Sometimes people send anonymous cards to someone they secretly admire.

April Fool's Day

1 April, is a day when people play jokes on each other until midday. Often TV and newspapers carry stories intended to deceive credulous viewers and readers.

Mother's Day

The Sunday three weeks before Easter is a day when children send cards or buy gifts for their mothers. Easter is also an important Christian festival.

Hallowe'en

31 October, is a very ancient festival. Young people will often dress up in frightening costumes to play 'trick or treat'. Giving them sweets or chocolates might stop them playing a trick on you. Sometimes people carry lanterns made out of pumpkins with a candle inside.

Guy Fawkes Night

5 November, is an occasion when people in Great Britain set off fireworks at home or in special displays. The origin of this celebration was an event in 1605, when a group of Catholics led by Guy Fawkes failed in their plan to kill the Protestant king with a bomb in the Houses of Parliament.

Remembrance Day

11 November, commemorates those who died fighting in World War 1, World War 2 and other wars. Many people wear poppies (a red flower) in memory of those who died. At 11 a.m. there is a two-minute silence.

❝11 November, commemorates those who died fighting in World War 1, World War 2 and other wars.❞

Study tip: Use visual prompts

One good way of helping your brain to retain information is through the use of repetition. Put key words and phrases on sticky notes and place these at strategic points around your home. If you read 'women got same voting rights as men in 1928' every time you open the fridge, this important date is more likely to stick in your memory.

SPORT

Sport of all kinds plays an important part in many people's lives. Football, tennis, rugby and cricket are very popular sports in the UK. There are no United Kingdom teams for football and rugby. England, Scotland, Wales and Northern Ireland have their own teams. Important sporting events include, the Grand National horse race, the Football Association (FA) cup final (and equivalents in Northern Ireland, Scotland and Wales), the Open golf championship and the Wimbledon tennis tournament.

Check that you understand
• Which sports are the most popular in the UK
• The patron saints' days in England, Scotland, Wales and Northern Ireland
• What Bank Holidays are
• The main traditional festivals in the UK
• That the main festivals in the UK are Christian based, but that important festivals from other religions are recognised and explained to children in schools

England, Scotland and Wales have their own rugby teams, but Northern Ireland does not. There is, however, a national football team for England, Scotland, Wales and Northern Ireland. For the purposes of the Life in the UK Test, you will need to learn the text as presented in the reproduced study chapters.

UK today: a profile

Practice questions

For the answers to these questions, see page 190.

1. **True or False? The English language sounds exactly the same wherever you go in the UK.**
   A True
   B False

2. **What was the total population of the United Kingdom in 2005?**
   A 49.8 million
   B 59.8 million
   C 69.8 million
   D 79.8 million

3. **What is the Church of England known as in Scotland and the USA?**
   A The Baptist Church
   B The Episcopal Church
   C The Anglican Church
   D The Protestant Church

4. **Which of these statements is correct?**
   A There has been a decline in population in the North-East of England
   B There has been an increase in population in the North-East of England

5. **There are TWO main Christian festivals celebrated in the UK. What are they? (Select two options)**
   A New Year's Eve
   B Mother's Day
   C Easter
   D Christmas

6. **True or False? The growth of the British population has been faster in more recent years.**
   A True
   B False

7. **What is a census?**
   A The valve connecting a dishwasher to the water line
   B A count of the whole population
   C A statement of how much income tax you have to pay
   D The person who decides the classification of a film

8. **Where is the Notting Hill Carnival held?**
   A Manchester
   B Liverpool
   C Birmingham
   D London

9 Which group of people form the largest ethnic minority group?

A Black Caribbean

B Indian

C Pakistani

D Bangladeshi

10 According to the 2001 census, what percentage of the people in the United Kingdom are of ethnic descent?

A 8.3%

B 18.3%

C 28.3%

D 38.3%

11 Since 2004, where have large numbers of immigrants come from?

A Afghanistan and Iraq

B Ethiopia and the Sudan

C The new East European member states of the European Union

D Southern Spain and Morocco

12 True or False? Boxing Day is when people return to work after Christmas.

A True

B False

13 Where is the Geordie dialect spoken?

A Liverpool

B London

C Tyneside

D Manchester

14 What area of England does NOT have a large ethnic minority population?

A Yorkshire and Humberside

B The South East

C West Midlands and the North West

D The South West

15 True or False? The UK has a record number of people aged 85 and over.

A True

B False

16 What are the National Saints of England, Scotland, Wales and Northern Ireland known as?

A Country Saints

B Patron Saints

C Holy Saints

D Guardian Saints

17 True or False? In Wales, Welsh is taught in schools and universities.

A True

B False

18 Which of the following statements is correct?

A Only licensed religions may be practised in the UK

B Everyone in the UK has the legal right to practise the religion of their choice

19 In the 2001 census, what proportion of the population said they had a religion?

A 25%

B 50%

C 75%

D 100%

20 How are non-Christian religious festivals treated?

A They are explained to children at school

B They are banned under British law

C They can only be celebrated in a licensed religious property

D They are celebrated by all faiths

21 True or False? All Patron Saints' days are public holidays.

A True

B False

22 What is traditionally exchanged on Valentine's Day?

A Chocolate eggs

B Pumpkin lanterns

C Red poppies

D Cards and gifts

23 What is the established church in Wales?

A The Presbyterian Church

B The Episcopal Church

C The Anglican Church

D There is no established church in Wales

24 Who is the most senior representative of the church in Scotland?

A The Queen

B The Pope

C The Moderator

D The Prime Minister

25 What percentage of the UK population stated that they were Muslim?

A 2.7%

B 5.7%

C 10.7%

D 15.7%

26 True or False? Non-Christians also celebrate Christmas.

A True

B False

27 What is 31 December called in Scotland?

A Hogwarts

B Hogmanay

C Hogshead

D Hogsback

28 What does Guy Fawkes night commemorate?

A A failed plan to kill the king

B The start of fireworks season

C The start of bonfire season

D The opening of Parliament

29 What does Remembrance Day commemorate?

A Those who died in the First World War

B Those who died in the Second World War

C Those who died in the Second World War and other wars

D Those who died in the First World War, Second World War and other wars

30 What is the Grand National?

A A theatre in London

B A major canal

C A horse race

D A royal palace

How the United Kingdom is governed

The UK's system of Government can seem complicated because it operates as a constitutional democracy with an unwritten constitution. This chapter reveals how the UK is governed and how its citizens take part in the process. It also looks beyond the UK to discuss its relationships with the European Union, the Commonwealth and the United Nations.

The British Constitution

The UK is governed by a parliamentary democracy directly involving the work of political parties, MPs and peers. Checks and balances on power in the UK are provided by a range of institutions.

In this section there is information about:
- The system of government
- The monarchy
- The electoral system
- Political parties
- Being a citizen
- Voting
- Contacting your MP

As a constitutional democracy, the United Kingdom is governed by a wide range of institutions, many of which provide checks on each other's powers. Most of these institutions are of long standing: they include the monarchy, Parliament (consisting of the House of Commons and the House of Lords), the office of Prime Minister, the Cabinet, the judiciary, the police, the civil service, and the institutions of local government. More recently, devolved administrations have been set up for Scotland, Wales and Northern Ireland. Together, these formal institutions, laws and conventions form the British Constitution. Some people would argue that the roles of other less formal institutions, such as the media and pressure groups, should also be seen as part of the Constitution.

The British Constitution is not written down in any single document, as are the constitutions of many other countries. This is mainly because the United Kingdom has never had a lasting revolution, like America or France, so our most important institutions have been in existence for hundreds of years. Some people believe that there should be a single document, but others believe that an unwritten constitution allows more scope for institutions to adapt to meet changing circumstances and public expectations.

THE MONARCHY

Queen Elizabeth II is the Head of State of the United Kingdom. She is also the monarch or Head of State for many countries in the Commonwealth. The UK, like Denmark, the Netherlands, Norway, Spain and Sweden, has a constitutional monarchy. This means that the king or queen does not rule the country, but appoints the government which the people have chosen in democratic elections. Although the queen or king can advise, warn and encourage the Prime Minister, the decisions on government policies are made by the Prime Minister and Cabinet.

The Queen has reigned since her father's death in 1952. Prince Charles, the Prince of Wales, her oldest son, is the heir to the throne.

The Queen has important ceremonial roles such as the opening of the new parliamentary session each year. On this occasion the Queen makes a speech that summarises the government's policies for the year ahead.

" Although the queen or king can advise, warn and encourage the Prime Minister, the decisions on government policies are made by the Prime Minister and Cabinet. "

GOVERNMENT

The system of government in the United Kingdom is a parliamentary democracy. The UK is divided into 646 parliamentary constituencies and at least every five years voters in each constituency elect their Member of Parliament (MP) in a general election. All of the elected MPs form the House of Commons. Most MPs belong to a political party and the party with the largest number of MPs forms the government.

The law that requires new elections to Parliament to be held at least every five years is so fundamental that no government has sought to change it. A Bill to change it is the only one to which the House of Lords must give its consent.

Some people argue that the power of Parliament is lessened because of the obligation on the United Kingdom to accept the rules of the European Union and the judgments of the European Court, but it was Parliament itself which created these obligations.

THE HOUSE OF COMMONS

The House of Commons is the more important of the two chambers in Parliament and its members are democratically elected. Nowadays the Prime Minister and almost all the members of the Cabinet are members of the House of Commons. The members of the House of Commons are called 'Members of Parliament' or MPs for short. Each MP represents a parliamentary constituency, or area of the country: there are 646 of these. MPs have a number of different responsibilities. They represent everyone in their constituency, they help to create new laws, they scrutinise and comment on what the government is doing, and they debate important national issues.

❝ Each MP represents a parliamentary constituency, or area of the country: there are 646 of these. ❞

ELECTIONS

There must be a general election to elect MPs at least every five years, though they may be held sooner if the Prime Minister so decides.

If an MP dies or resigns, there will be another election, called a by-election, in his or her constituency. MPs are elected through a system called 'first past the post'. In each constituency, the candidate who gets the most votes is elected. The government is then formed by the party which wins the majority of constituencies.

THE WHIPS

The Whips are a small group of MPs appointed by their party leaders. They are responsible for discipline in their party and making sure MPs attend the House of Commons to vote. The Chief Whip often attends Cabinet or Shadow Cabinet meetings and arranges the schedule of proceedings in the House of Commons with the Speaker.

EUROPEAN PARLIAMENTARY ELECTIONS

Elections for the European Parliament are also held every five years. There are 78 seats for representatives from the UK in the European Parliament and elected members are called Members of the European

Parliament (MEPs). Elections to the European Parliament use a system of proportional representation, whereby seats are allocated to each party in proportion to the total votes it won.

THE HOUSE OF LORDS

Members of the House of Lords, known as peers, are not elected and do not represent a constituency. The role and membership of the House of Lords have recently undergone big changes. Until 1958 all peers were either 'hereditary' meaning that their titles were inherited, senior judges, or bishops of the Church of England. Since 1958 the Prime Minister has had the power to appoint peers just for their own lifetime. These peers, known as Life Peers, have usually had a distinguished career in politics, business, law or some other profession. This means that debates in the House of Lords often draw on more specialist knowledge than is available to members of the House of Commons. Life Peers are appointed by the Queen on the advice of the Prime Minister but they include people nominated by the leaders of the other main parties and by an independent Appointments Commission for non-party peers.

In the last few years the hereditary peers have lost the automatic right to attend the House of Lords, although they are allowed to elect a few of their number to represent them.

While the House of Lords is usually the less important of the two chambers of Parliament, it is more independent of the government. It can suggest amendments or propose new laws, which are then discussed by the House of Commons. The House of Lords can become very important if the majority of its members will not agree to pass a law for which the House of Commons has voted. The House of Commons has powers to overrule the House of Lords, but these are very rarely used.

THE PRIME MINISTER

The Prime Minister (PM) is the leader of the political party in power. He or she appoints the members of the Cabinet and has control over many important public appointments. The official home of the Prime Minister is 10 Downing Street, in central London, near the Houses of Parliament; he or she also has a country house not far from London called Chequers. The Prime Minister can be changed if the MPs in the governing party decide to do so, or if he or she wishes to resign. More usually, the Prime Minister resigns when his or her party is defeated in a general election.

"The Leader of the Opposition is the person who hopes to become Prime Minister if his or her party wins the next general election. "

THE CABINET

The Prime Minister appoints about 20 senior MPs to become ministers in charge of departments. These include the Chancellor of the Exchequer, responsible for the economy, the Home Secretary, responsible for law, order and immigration, the Foreign Secretary, and ministers (called 'Secretaries of State') for education, health and defence. The Lord Chancellor, who is the minister responsible for legal affairs, is also a member of the Cabinet but sat in the House of Lords rather than the House of Commons. Following legislation passed in 2005, it is now possible for the Lord Chancellor to sit in the Commons. These ministers form the Cabinet, a small committee which usually meets weekly and makes important decisions about government policy which often then have to be debated or approved by Parliament.

THE OPPOSITION

The second largest party in the House of Commons is called the Opposition. The Leader of the Opposition is the person who hopes to become Prime Minister if his or her party wins the next general election. The Leader of the Opposition leads his or her party in pointing out the government's failures and weaknesses; one important opportunity to do this is at Prime Minister's Questions which takes place every week while Parliament is sitting. The Leader of the Opposition also appoints senior Opposition MPs to lead the criticism of government ministers, and together they form the Shadow Cabinet.

THE SPEAKER

Debates in the House of Commons are chaired by the Speaker, the chief officer of the House of Commons. The Speaker is politically neutral. He or she is an MP, elected by fellow MPs to keep order during political debates and to make sure the rules are followed. This includes making sure the Opposition has a guaranteed amount of time to debate issues it chooses. The Speaker also represents Parliament at ceremonial occasions.

"Pressure and lobby groups are organisations that try to influence government policy. They play a very important role in politics."

THE PARTY SYSTEM

Under the British system of parliamentary democracy, anyone can stand for election as an MP but they are unlikely to win an election unless they have been nominated to represent one of the major political parties. These are the Labour Party, the Conservative Party, the Liberal Democrats, or one of the parties representing Scottish, Welsh, or Northern Irish interests. There are just a few MPs who do not represent any of the main political parties and are called 'independents'. The main political parties actively seek members among ordinary voters to join their debates, contribute to their costs, and help at elections for Parliament or for local government; they have branches in most constituencies and they hold policy-making conferences every year.

PRESSURE AND LOBBY GROUPS

Pressure and lobby groups are organisations that try to influence government policy. They play a very important role in politics. There are many pressure groups in the UK. They may represent economic interests (such as the Confederation of British Industry, the Consumers' Association [Which?], or the trade unions) or views on particular subjects (e.g. Greenpeace or Liberty). The general public is more likely to support pressure groups than join a political party.

THE CIVIL SERVICE

Civil servants are managers and administrators who carry out government policy. They have to be politically neutral and professional, regardless of which political party is in power. Although civil servants have to follow the policies of the elected government, they can warn ministers if they think a policy is impractical or not in the public interest. Before a general election takes place, top civil servants study the Opposition party's policies closely in case they need to be ready to serve a new government with different aims and policies.

DEVOLVED ADMINISTRATION

In order to give people in Wales and Scotland more control of matters that directly affect them, in 1997 the government began a programme of devolving power from central government. Since 1999 there has been a Welsh Assembly, a Scottish Parliament and, periodically, a Northern Ireland Assembly. Although policy and laws governing defence, foreign affairs, taxation and social security all remain under central UK government control, many other public services now come under the control of the devolved administrations in Wales and Scotland.

Both the Scottish Parliament and Welsh Assembly have been set up using forms of proportional representation which ensures that each party gets a number of seats in proportion to the number of votes they receive. Similarly, proportional representation is used in Northern Ireland in order to ensure 'power sharing' between the Unionist majority (mainly Protestant) and the substantial (mainly Catholic) minority aligned to Irish nationalist parties. A different form of proportional representation is used for elections to the European Parliament.

ᶜᶜ Since 1999 there has been a Welsh Assembly, a Scottish Parliament and, periodically, a Northern Ireland Assembly. ᵗᵗ

THE WELSH ASSEMBLY GOVERNMENT

The National Assembly for Wales, or Welsh Assembly Government (WAG), is situated in Cardiff the capital city of Wales. It has 60 Assembly Members (AMs) and elections are held every four years. Members can speak in either Welsh or English and all its publications are in both languages. The Assembly has the power to make decisions on important matters such as education policy, the environment, health services, transport and local government, and to pass laws for Wales on these matters within a statutory framework set out by the UK Parliament at Westminster.

THE PARLIAMENT OF SCOTLAND

A long campaign in Scotland for more independence and democratic control led to the formation in 1999 of the Parliament of Scotland, which sits in Edinburgh, the capital city of Scotland.

There are 129 Members of the Scottish Parliament (MSPs), elected by a form of proportional representation. This has led to the sharing of power in Scotland between the Labour and Liberal Democrat parties. The Scottish Parliament can pass legislation for Scotland on all matters that are not specifically reserved to the UK Parliament. The matters on which the Scottish Parliament can legislate include civil and criminal law, health, education, planning and the raising of additional taxes.

THE NORTHERN IRELAND ASSEMBLY

A Northern Ireland Parliament was established in 1922 when Ireland was divided, but it was abolished in 1972 shortly after the Troubles broke out in 1969.

Soon after the end of the Troubles, the Northern Ireland Assembly was established with a power-sharing agreement which distributes ministerial offices among the main parties. The Assembly has 108 elected members known as MLAs (Members of the Legislative Assembly). Decision-making powers devolved to Northern Ireland include education, agriculture, the environment, health and social services in Northern Ireland.

The UK government kept the power to suspend the Northern Ireland Assembly if the political leaders no longer agreed to work together or if the Assembly was not working in the interests of the people of Northern Ireland. This has happened several times and the Assembly is currently suspended (2006). This means that the elected assembly members do not have power to pass bills or make decisions.

Full power was restored to the Northern Ireland Assembly in May 2007. For the purposes of the current UK citizenship test, however, you will be asked questions based on the text of the book, *Life in the United Kingdom: A Journey to Citizenship*. This was published before the Northern Ireland Assembly was restored.

LOCAL GOVERNMENT

Towns, cities and rural areas in the UK are governed by democratically elected councils, often called local authorities. Some areas have both district and county councils which have different functions, although most larger towns and cities will have a single local authority. Many councils representing towns and cities appoint a mayor who is the ceremonial leader of the council but in some towns a mayor is appointed to be the effective leader of the administration. London has 33 local authorities, with the Greater London Authority and the Mayor of London co-ordinating policies across the capital. Local authorities are required to provide 'mandatory services' in their area. These services include education, housing, social services, passenger transport, the fire service, rubbish collection, planning, environmental health and libraries.

Most of the money for the local authority services comes from the government through taxes. Only about 20% is funded locally through 'council tax' a local tax set by councils to help pay for local services. It applies to all domestic properties, including houses, bungalows, flats, maisonettes, mobile homes or houseboats, whether owned or rented.

Local elections for councillors are held in May every year. Many candidates stand for council election as members of a political party.

Study tip: Use memory techniques

Our brains respond well to different 'tricks' to help us remember things. Experiment with a range of techniques and work out what works best for you. For example, you might want to make notes on women in pink – this use of colour may help you remember them when you try to recall women's issues later. You could also try rhymes, word association and mnemonics. Mnemonics are words or phrases that are created from the first letter of a list of other words. For example, you may want to remember the three most important agreements produced by the UN: the Universal Declaration of Human Rights, the Convention on the Elimination of All Forms of Discrimination against Women, and the UN Convention on the Rights of the Child. Your new, funny and easy to remember sentence may then read: Ursula Dines on Hot Rice, Charlie only Eats Apples, Fried Dumplings and Walnuts and Umpire Nick Consumes only the Ripest Cheese.

THE JUDICIARY

In the UK the laws made by Parliament are the highest authority. But often important questions arise about how the laws are to be interpreted in particular cases. It is the task of the judges (who are together called 'the judiciary') to interpret the law, and the government may not interfere with their role. Often the actions of the government are claimed to be illegal and, if the judges agree, then the government must either change its policies or ask Parliament to change the law. This has become all the more important in recent years, as the judges now have the task of applying the Human Rights Act. If they find that a public body is not respecting a person's human rights, they may order that body to change its practices and to pay compensation, if appropriate. If the judges believe that an Act of Parliament is incompatible with the Human Rights Act, they cannot change it themselves but they can ask Parliament to consider doing so.

Judges cannot, however, decide whether people are guilty or innocent of serious crimes. When someone is accused of a serious crime, a jury will decide whether he or she is innocent or guilty and, if guilty, the judge will decide on the penalty. For less important crimes, a magistrate will decide on guilt and on any penalty.

THE POLICE

The police service is organised locally, with one police service for each county or group of counties. The largest force is the Metropolitan Police, which serves London and is based at New Scotland Yard. Northern Ireland as a whole is served by the Police Service for Northern Ireland (PSNI). The police have 'operational independence', which means that the government cannot instruct them on what to do in any particular case. But the powers of the police are limited by the law and their finances are controlled by the government and by police authorities made up of councillors and magistrates. The Independent Police Complaints Commission (or, in Northern Ireland, the Police Ombudsman) investigates serious complaints against the police.

NON-DEPARTMENTAL PUBLIC BODIES (QUANGOS)

Non-departmental public bodies, also known as quangos, are independent organisations that carry out functions on behalf of the public which it would be inappropriate to place under the political control of a Cabinet minister. There are many hundreds of these bodies, carrying out a wide variety of

63

public duties. Appointments to these bodies are usually made by ministers, but they must do so in an open and fair way.

THE ROLE OF THE MEDIA

Proceedings in Parliament are broadcast on digital television and published in official reports such as Hansard, which is available in large libraries and on the Internet: www.parliament.uk. Most people, however, get information about political issues and events from newspapers (often called the press), television and radio.

The UK has a free press, meaning that what is written in newspapers is free from government control. Newspaper owners and editors hold strong political opinions and run campaigns to try and influence government policy and public opinion. As a result it is sometimes difficult to distinguish fact from opinion in newspaper coverage.

By law, radio and television coverage of the political parties at election periods must be balanced and so equal time has to be given to rival viewpoints. But broadcasters are free to interview politicians in a tough and lively way.

❝ Newspaper owners and editors hold strong political opinions and run campaigns to try and influence government policy and public opinion. ❞

WHO CAN VOTE?

The United Kingdom has had a fully democratic system since 1928, when women were allowed to vote at 21, the same age as men. The present voting age of 18 was set in 1969, and (with a few exceptions such as convicted prisoners) all UK-born and naturalised citizens have full civic rights, including the right to vote and do jury service.

Citizens of the UK, the Commonwealth and the Irish Republic (if resident in the UK) can vote in all public elections. Citizens of EU states who are resident in the UK can vote in all elections except national parliamentary (general) elections.

 Voter registration forms are available online. For further information see www.electoralcommission.org.uk

In order to vote in a parliamentary, local or European election, you must have your name on the register of electors, known as the electoral register. If you are eligible to vote, you can register by contacting your local council election registration office. If you don't know what your local authority is, you can find out by telephoning the Local Government Association (LGA) information line on 020 7664 3131 between 9am and 5pm, Monday to Friday. You will have to tell them your postcode or your full address and they will be able to give you the name of your local authority. You can also get voter registration forms in English, Welsh and some other languages on the internet: www.electoralcommission.org.uk

The electoral register is updated every year in September or October. An electoral registration form is sent to every household and it has to be completed and returned, with the names of everyone who is resident in the household and eligible to vote on 15 October.

In Northern Ireland a different system operates. This is called individual registration and all those entitled to vote must complete their own registration form. Once registered, you can stay on the register provided your personal details do not change. For more information telephone the Electoral Office for Northern Ireland on 028 9044 6688.

By law, each local authority has to make its electoral register available for anyone to look at, although this now has to be supervised. The register is kept at each local electoral registration office (or council office in England and Wales). It is also possible to see the register at some public buildings such as libraries.

STANDING FOR OFFICE

Most citizens of the United Kingdom, the Irish Republic or the Commonwealth aged 18 or over can stand for public office. There are some exceptions and these include members of the armed forces, civil servants and people found guilty of certain criminal offences. Members of the House of Lords may not stand for election to the House of Commons but are eligible for all other public offices.

To become a local councillor, a candidate must have a local connection with the area through work, being on the electoral register, or through renting or owning land or property.

 For further information on how to find out the name of your local MP and how to contact them, see www.writetothem.com. For information on visiting the Houses of Parliament see www.parliament.uk

CONTACTING ELECTED MEMBERS

All elected members have a duty to serve and represent their constituents. You can get contact details for all your representatives and their parties from your local library. Assembly members, MSPs, MPs and MEPs are also listed in the phone book and Yellow Pages. You can contact MPs by letter or phone at their constituency office or their office in the House of Commons: The House of Commons, Westminster, London SW1A OAA, or telephone: O2O 7729 3OOO. Many Assembly Members, MSPs, MPs and MEPs hold regular local 'surgeries'. These are often advertised in the local paper and constituents can go and talk about issues in person. You can find out the name of your local MP and get in touch with them by fax through the website: www.writetothem.com. This service is free.

HOW TO VISIT PARLIAMENT AND THE DEVOLVED ADMINISTRATIONS

- The public can listen to debates in the Palace of Westminster from public galleries in both the House of Commons and the House of Lords. You can either write to your local MP in advance to ask for tickets or you can queue on the day at the public entrance. Entrance is free. Sometimes there are long queues for the House of Commons and you may have to wait for at least one or two hours. It is usually easier to get into the House of Lords. You can find further information on the UK Parliament website: www.parliament.uk

" The public can listen to debates in the Palace of Westminster from public galleries in both the House of Commons and the House of Lords. "

- In Northern Ireland, elected members, known as MLAs, meet in the Northern Ireland Assembly at Stormont, in Belfast. The Northern Ireland Assembly is presently suspended. There are two ways to arrange a visit to Stormont. You can either contact the Education Service (details on the Northern Ireland Assembly website: www.niassembly.gov.uk) or contact an MLA.

- In Scotland, the elected members, called MSPs, meet in the Scottish Parliament at Holyrood in Edinburgh (for more information see: www.scottish.parliament.uk). You can get information, book tickets or arrange tours through the visitor services. You can write to them at The Scottish Parliament, Edinburgh, EH99 1SP, or telephone 0131 348 5200, or email sp.bookings@scottish.parliament.uk

- In Wales, the elected members, known as AMs, meet in the Welsh Assembly in the Senedd in Cardiff Bay (for more information see: www.wales.gov.uk). You can book guided tours or seats in the public galleries for the Welsh Assembly. To make a booking, telephone the Assembly booking line on 029 2089 8477 or email: assembly.booking@wales.gsi.gov.uk

Check that you understand
- The role of the monarchy
- How parliament works, and the difference between the House of Commons and the House of Lords
- How often general elections are held
- Where the official residence of the Prime Minister is
- The role of the Cabinet and who is in it
- The nature of the UK Constitution
- The job of the Opposition, the Leader of the Opposition and the Shadow Cabinet
- The difference between 'first past the post' and proportional representation
- The form of electoral systems in the devolved administrations in Northern Ireland, Scotland and Wales
- The rights and duties of British citizens, including naturalised citizens
- How the judiciary, police and local authorities work
- What non-departmental public bodies are

For further information on the Northern Ireland Assembly, see www.niassembly.gov.uk
For the Scottish Parliament, see www.scottish.parliament.uk
And find more on the Welsh Assembly at www.wales.gov.uk

The UK in Europe and the world

The UK is a member of several world organisations. These include the European Union, the Commonwealth and the United Nations. This section provides an overview of these organisations and the UK's role within them.

In this chapter there is information about:
- The UK in Europe and the world
- The European Union
- The Commonwealth
- The United Nations

THE COMMONWEALTH

The Commonwealth is an association of countries, most of which were once part of the British Empire, though a few countries that were not in the Empire have also joined it.

Commonwealth members

Antigua and	Ghana	New Zealand	South Africa
Barbuda	Grenada	Nigeria	Sri Lanka
Australia	Guyana	Pakistan	Swaziland
The Bahamas	India	Papua New	Tonga
Bangladesh	Jamaica	Guinea	Trinidad and
Barbados	Kenya	St Kitts and	Tobago
Belize	Kiribati	Nevis	Tuvalu
Botswana	Lesotho	St Lucia	Uganda
Brunei	Malawi	St Vincent	United Kingdom
Darussalam	Malaysia	and the	United Republic
Cameroon	Maldives	Grenadines	of Tanzania
Canada	Malta	Samoa	Vanuatu
Cyprus	Mauritius	Seychelles	Zambia
Dominica	Mozambique	Sierra Leone	
Fiji Islands	Namibia	Singapore	*Nauru is a*
The Gambia	Nauru*	Solomon Islands	*Special Member*

Study tip: Make friends

It can help to study with a friend. You can talk to each other about areas you don't understand and share tips on how to remember facts. Use the practice questions to test each other. You can also spur yourselves on if you get stuck and encourage each other to keep revising.

The Queen is the head of the Commonwealth, which currently has 53 member states. Membership is voluntary and the Commonwealth has no power over its members although it can suspend membership. The Commonwealth aims to promote democracy, good government and to eradicate poverty.

THE EUROPEAN UNION (EU)

The European Union (EU), originally called the European Economic Community (EEC), was set up by six Western European countries who signed the Treaty of Rome on 25 March 1957. One of the main reasons for doing this was the belief that co-operation between states would reduce the likelihood of another war in Europe. Originally the UK decided not to join this group and only became part of the European Union in 1973. In 2004 ten new member countries joined the EU, with a further two in 2006 making a total of 27 member countries.

One of the main aims of the EU today is for member states to function as a single market. Most of the countries of the EU have a shared currency, the euro, but the UK has decided to retain its own currency unless the British people choose to accept the euro in a referendum. Citizens of an EU member state have the right to travel to and work in any EU country if they have a valid passport or identity card. This right can be restricted on the grounds of public health, public order and public security. The right to work is also sometimes restricted for citizens of countries that have joined the EU recently.

> **!** The EU's newest members, Romania and Bulgaria, joined on 1 January 2007, not 2006 as stated in the official Home Office text. For the purposes of the Life in the UK Test, however, you will need to learn the official text.

The Council of the European Union (usually called the Council of Ministers) is effectively the governing body of the EU. It is made up of government ministers from each country in the EU and, together with the European Parliament, is the legislative body of the EU. The Council of Ministers passes EU law on the recommendations of the European Commission and the European Parliament and takes the most important decisions about how the EU is run. The European Commission is based in Brussels, the capital city of Belgium. It is the civil service of the EU and drafts proposals for new EU policies and laws and administers its funding programmes.

The European Parliament meets in Strasbourg, in north-eastern France, and in Brussels. Each country elects members, called Members of the European Parliament (MEPs), every five years. The European Parliament examines decisions made by the European Council and the European Commission, and it has the power to refuse agreement to European laws proposed by the commission and to check on the spending of EU funds.

European Union law is legally binding in the UK and all the other member states. European laws, called directives, regulations or framework decisions, have made a lot of difference to people's rights in the UK, particularly at work. For example, there are EU directives about the procedures for making workers redundant and regulations that limit the number of hours people can be made to work.

Study tip: Relax!

Panic could distract you during your test. Practice relaxation techniques while revising, so you are familiar with them when sit your test.
Start with a deep breath, hold it for a moment and then exhale slowly. Think about where you are holding tension, such as your shoulders or your jaw. Concentrate on relaxing this and repeat the breathing exercise.

THE COUNCIL OF EUROPE

The Council of Europe was created in 1949 and the UK was one of the founder members. Most of the countries of Europe are members. It has no power to make laws but draws up conventions and charters which focus on human rights, democracy, education, the environment, health and culture. The most important of these is the European Convention on Human Rights;

all member states are bound by this Convention and a member state which persistently refuses to obey the Convention may be expelled from the Council of Europe.

THE UNITED NATIONS (UN)

The UK is a member of the United Nations (UN), an international organisation to which over 190 countries now belong. The UN was set up after the Second World War and aims to prevent war and promote international peace and security. There are 15 members on the UN Security Council, which recommends action by the UN when there are international crises and threats to peace. The UK is one of the five permanent members.

Three very important agreements produced by the UN are the Universal Declaration of Human Rights, the Convention on the Elimination of All Forms of Discrimination against Women, and the UN Convention on the Rights of the Child. Although none of these has the force of law, they are widely used in political debate and legal cases to reinforce the law and to assess the behaviour of countries.

❝ There are 15 members on the UN Security Council, which recommends action by the UN when there are international crises and threats to peace. ❞

Check that you understand
- The differences between the Council of Europe, the European Union, the European Commission and the European Parliament
- The UK is a member of the Council of Europe and the European Union
- The EU aims to become a single market and it is administered by a Council of Ministers of governments of member states
- Subject to some restrictions, EU citizens may travel to and work in any EU country
- The roles of the UN and the Commonwealth

How the United Kingdom is governed

Practice questions

For the answers to these questions, see page 190.

1 Which is NOT one of the institutions that provide checks on the British system of Government?

A The Cabinet
B The judiciary
C The police
D Television

2 True or False? As with many other countries, Britain has a written Constitution.

A True
B False

3 What type of monarchy does the UK have?

A A ceremonial monarchy
B A constitutional monarchy
C A democratic monarchy
D An absolute monarchy

4 What important ceremonial role does the king or queen perform?

A Voting in the House of Commons
B Meeting weekly with the Prime Minister
C Opening of a new parliamentary session each year
D Chairing proceedings in the House of Lords

5 How often are general elections held in Britain?

A At least every 4 years
B At least every 5 years
C At least every 6 years
D At least every 7 years

6 What is an MP?

A A Mile Post
B A Member of Parliament
C A member of the Manchester Police
D A member of the Metropolitan Police

7 Who forms the Government?

A The party that wins the majority of constituencies
B The party that wins the greatest number of votes
C The party instructed by the Queen to form the Government
D The party whose leader wins the greatest number of votes

8 What is the second largest party in the House of Commons called?

A The Opposition
B The Backbench
C The Otherside
D The Defence

9 What does PM stand for?

A Process Manager

B Prime Minister

C Post Meridian

D Post Master

10 Which is not a political party in Britain?

A The Labour Party

B The Conservative Party

C The Liberal Democrats

D The Independents

11 True or False? The civil service is politically neutral.

A True

B False

12 By what system are Members of the Scottish Parliament, Welsh Assembly and Northern Ireland Assembly elected?

A Instant runoff

B First past the post

C Proportional representation

D Multiseat representation

13 What are Members of the Scottish Parliament called?

A MSPs (Members of the Scottish Parliament)

B SMPs (Scottish Parliamentary Members)

C Members of the SP

D MPSs (Members of the Parliament of Scotland)

14 Who administers towns, cities and rural areas in Britain?

A The police

B Local Authorities

C The civil service

D Parliament

15 What is council tax?

A It is money used to pay for local elections

B It is a tax you must pay when you buy a new house

C A reduced rate of tax that council employees pay on their wages

D A local tax set by councils to help pay for local services

16 True or False? Judges interpret the law.

A True

B False

17 What is a quango?

A A semi-independent agency chaired by the Prime Minister

B A part of the governing structure of the European Parliament

C A non-departmental public body

D A commission appointed by the monarch

18 In which area have EU laws made a great difference to life in the UK?

A Accommodation

B Health

C Travel

D Work

19 Which of these statements is correct?

A Both UK born and naturalised citizens have the right to vote

B Only UK born citizens have the right to vote

20 What currency do several of the countries of the EU share?

A The dollar

B The euro

C The ECU

D The pound

21 Which of these statements is correct?

A The United Kingdom has to accept the rules of the European Union

B The United Kingdom can ignore the rules of the European Union

---

22 True or False? Most members of the Commonwealth were once part of the British Empire.

A True

B False

---

23 How many members made up the European Union in 2006?

A 17 states

B 27 states

C 37 states

D 47 states

---

24 True or False? People standing for election as a local councillor are never members of a political party.

A True

B False

---

25 How often does Prime Minister's Questions take place?

A Daily

B Weekly

C Monthly

D Yearly

---

26 True or False? Citizens of an EU member state do NOT have the right to travel to and work in any EU country if they have a valid passport or identity card.

A True

B False

---

27 What kind of administration has recently been set up for Scotland, Wales and Northern Ireland?

A Involved

B Revolved

C Devolved

D Solved

---

28 True or False? The UK is one of the five permanent members of the UN Security Council.

A True

B False

---

29 Who is the Prince of Wales?

A Prince Philip

B Prince Charles

C Prince Andrew

D Prince Edward

---

30 Do documents produced by the United Nations have the force of law?

A Yes

B No

Everyday needs

Day-to-day life in the UK may involve setting up a new home, finding a doctor and exploring a variety of leisure activities. You will probably want to get out and about, possibly through the use of different transport options. Even these simple activities can be daunting in a new country which may use different procedures than you are used to. This chapter explores what you need to know in order to make your everyday needs easy.

Housing

Whether you are buying or renting your home in the UK, there are certain procedures you must complete. This ranges from signing a contract or tenancy agreement to organising support such as Housing Benefit if necessary.

In this section there is information about:
- Housing

BUYING A HOME

Two-thirds of people in the UK own their own home. Most other people rent houses, flats or rooms.

MORTGAGES

People who buy their own home usually pay for it with a mortgage, a special loan from a bank or building society. This loan is paid back, with interest, over a long period of time, usually 25 years. You can get information about mortgages from a bank or building society. Some banks can also give information about Islamic (Sharia) mortgages.

If you are having problems paying your mortgage repayments, you can get help and advice (see Help page 80). It is important to speak to your bank or building society as soon as you can.

ESTATE AGENTS

If you wish to buy a home, usually the first place to start is an estate agent. In Scotland the process is different and you should go first to a solicitor. Estate agents represent the person selling their house or flat. They arrange for buyers to visit homes that are for sale. There are estate agents in all towns and cities and they usually have websites where they advertise

 For information and advice on buying, selling and moving home, see the Which? Essential Guide *Buy, Sell and Move House.*

the homes for sale. You can also find details about homes for sale on the internet and in national and local newspapers.

MAKING AN OFFER

In the UK, except in Scotland, when you find a home you wish to buy you have to make an offer to the seller. You usually do this through an estate agent or solicitor. Many people offer a lower price than the seller is asking. Your first offer must be 'subject to contract' so that you can withdraw if there are reasons why you cannot complete the purchase. In Scotland the seller sets a price and buyers make offers over that amount. The agreement becomes legally binding earlier than it does elsewhere in the UK.

SOLICITOR AND SURVEYOR

It is important that a solicitor helps you through the process of buying a house or flat. When you make an offer on a property, the solicitor will carry out a number of legal checks on the property, the seller and the local area. The solicitor will provide the legal agreements necessary for you to buy the property. The bank or building society that is providing you with your mortgage will also carry out checks on the house or flat you wish to buy. These are done by a surveyor. The buyer does not usually see the result of this survey, so the buyer often asks a second surveyor to check the house as well. In Scotland the survey is carried out before an offer is made, to help people decide how much they want to bid for the property.

" When you make an offer on a property, your solicitor will carry out a number of legal checks on the property, the seller and the local area. "

RENTED ACCOMMODATION

It is possible to rent accommodation from the local authority (the council), from a housing association or from private property owners called landlords.

THE LOCAL AUTHORITY

Most local authorities (or councils) provide housing. This is often called 'council housing'. In Northern Ireland social housing is provided by the Northern Ireland Housing Executive (www.nihe.co.uk). In Scotland you can find information on social housing at: www.sfha.co.uk. Everyone is entitled to apply for council accommodation. To apply you must put your name on the council register or list. This is available from the housing department at the local authority. You are then assessed according to your needs. This is done through a system of points. You get more points if you have priority needs, for example if you are homeless and have children or chronic ill health.

It is important to note that in many areas of the UK there is a shortage of council accommodation, and that some people have to wait a very long time for a house or flat.

HOUSING ASSOCIATIONS

Housing associations are independent not-for-profit organisations which provide housing for rent. In some areas they have taken over the administration of local authority housing. They also run schemes called shared ownership, which help people buy part of a house or flat if they cannot afford to buy all of it at once. There are usually waiting lists for homes owned by housing associations.

PRIVATELY RENTED ACCOMMODATION

Many people rent houses or flats privately, from landlords. Information about private accommodation can be found in local newspapers, notice boards, estate agents and letting agents.

 For further information on Housing Benefit and, if you rent from a private landlord, Local Housing Allowance, see www.direct.gov.uk. Additional sources of information are listed under Help on page 80.

TENANCY AGREEMENT

When you rent a house or flat privately you sign a tenancy agreement, or lease. This explains the conditions or 'rules' you must follow while renting the property. This agreement must be checked very carefully to avoid problems later. The agreement also contains a list of any furniture or fittings in the property. This is called an inventory. Before you sign the agreement check the details and keep it safe during your tenancy.

DEPOSIT AND RENT

You will probably be asked to give the landlord a deposit at the beginning of your tenancy. This is to cover the cost of any damage. It is usually equal to one month's rent. The landlord must return this money to you at the end of your tenancy, unless you have caused damage to the property.

Your rent is fixed with your landlord at the beginning of the tenancy. The landlord cannot raise the rent without your agreement.

If you have a low income or are unemployed you may be able to claim Housing Benefit (see Help page 80) to help you pay your rent.

❝Your landlord must return your deposit to you at the end of your tenancy, unless you have caused damage to the property.❞

RENEWING AND ENDING A TENANCY

Your tenancy agreement will be for a fixed period of time, often six months. After this time the tenancy can be ended or, if both tenant and landlord agree, renewed. If you end the tenancy before the fixed time, you usually have to pay the rent for the agreed full period of the tenancy.

A landlord cannot force a tenant to leave. If a landlord wishes a tenant to leave they must follow the correct procedures. These vary according to the type of tenancy. It is a criminal offence for a landlord to use threats or violence against a tenant or to force them to leave without an order from court.

DISCRIMINATION

It is unlawful for a landlord to discriminate against someone looking for accommodation because of their sex, race, nationality, or ethnic group, or because they are disabled, unless the landlord or a close relative of the landlord is sharing the accommodation.

HOMELESSNESS

If you are homeless you should go for help to the local authority (or, in Northern Ireland, the Housing Executive). They have a legal duty to offer help and advice, but will not offer you a place to live unless you have priority need (see The local authority on page 78) and have a connection with the area, such as work or family. You must also show that you have not made yourself intentionally homeless.

HELP

If you are homeless or have problems with your landlord, help can be found from the following:

- The housing department of the local authority will give advice on homelessness and on Housing Benefit as well as deal with problems you may have in council-owned property.
- The Citizens Advice Bureau will give advice on all types of housing problems. There may also be a housing advice centre in your neighbourhood.
- Shelter is a housing charity which runs a 24-hour helpline on 0808 800 4444, or visit www.shelternet.org.uk
- Help with the cost of moving and setting up home may be available from the Social Fund. This is run by the Department for Work and Pensions (DWP). It provides grants and loans such as the Community Care Grant for people setting up home after being homeless or after they have been in prison or other institutions. Other loans are available for people who have had an emergency such as flooding. Information about these is available at the Citizens Advice Bureau or Jobcentre Plus.

Study tip: Timing

Think carefully about how long you have to do the test. You will need to answer 24 questions in 45 minutes. This means you will have a little over one and a half minutes for each question. This is actually a long time if you have revised the text carefully, as you will probably know most answers instantly. Take your time over each question though. There is no need to rush.

Services in and for the home

This section gives an overview on the practicalities of living in the UK. Specifically, this comprises organising your utilities, including water, electricity and gas, arranging your home insurance and paying your household bills, including council tax.

In this section there is information about:
- Services in and for the home

WATER

Water is supplied to all homes in the UK. The charge for this is called the water rates. When you move in to a new home (bought or rented), you should receive a letter telling you the name of the company responsible for supplying your water. The water rates may be paid in one payment (a lump sum) or in instalments, usually monthly. If you receive Housing Benefit, you should check to see if this covers the water rates. The cost of the water usually depends on the size of your property, but some homes have a water meter which tells you exactly how much water you have used. In Northern Ireland water is currently (2006) included in the domestic rates (see Council tax on page 83), although this may change in future.

ELECTRICITY AND GAS

All properties in the UK have electricity supplied at 240 volts. Most homes also have gas. When you move into a new home or leave an old one, you should make a note of the electricity and gas meter readings. If you have an urgent problem with your gas, electricity or water supply, you can ring a 24-hour helpline. This can be found on your bill, in the *Yellow Pages* or in the phone book.

 New arrangements for the delivery of water and sewerage services came into operation in Northern Ireland on 1 April 2007. For the purposes of the current UK citizenship test, however, you will be asked questions based on this text, which is taken from the book, *Life in the United Kingdom: A Journey to Citizenship*. This was published before the new water arrangements were brought in.

GAS AND ELECTRICITY SUPPLIERS

It is possible to choose between different gas and electricity suppliers. These have different prices and different terms and conditions. Get advice before you sign a contract with a new supplier. To find out which company supplies your gas, telephone Transco on 0870 608 1524.

To find out which company supplies your electricity, telephone Energywatch on 0845 906 0708 or visit www.energywatch.org.uk. Energywatch can also give you advice on changing your supplier of electricity or gas.

TELEPHONE

Most homes already have a telephone line (called a land line). If you need a new line, telephone BT on 150 442, or contact a cable company. Many companies offer land line, mobile telephone and broadband internet services. You can get advice about prices or about changing your company from Ofcom at www.ofcom.org.uk. You can call from public payphones using cash, pre-paid phonecards or credit or debit cards. Calls made from hotels and hostels are usually more expensive. Dial 999 or 112 for emergency calls for police, fire or ambulance service. These calls are free. Do not use these numbers if it is not a real emergency; you can always find the local numbers for these services in the phone book.

BILLS

Information on how to pay for water, gas, electricity and the telephone is found on the back of each bill. If you have a bank account you can pay your bills by standing order or direct debit. Most companies operate a budget scheme which allows you to pay a fixed sum every month. If you do not pay a bill, the service can be cut off. To get a service reconnected, you have to pay another charge.

❝In many places you must recycle your rubbish, separating paper, glass, metal or plastic from the other rubbish.❞

REFUSE COLLECTION

Refuse is also called waste, or rubbish. The local authority collects the waste regularly, usually on the same day of each week. Waste must be put outside in a particular place to get collected. In some parts of the country the waste is put into plastic bags, in others it is put into bins with wheels. In many places you must recycle your rubbish, separating paper, glass, metal or plastic from the other rubbish. Large objects which you want to throw away, such as a bed, a wardrobe or a fridge, need to be collected separately. Contact the local authority to arrange this. If you have a business, such as a factory or a shop, you must make special arrangements with the local authority for your waste to be collected. It is a criminal offence to dump rubbish anywhere.

COUNCIL TAX

Local government services, such as education, police, roads, refuse collection and libraries, are paid for partly by grants from the government and partly by Council Tax. In Northern Ireland there is a system of domestic rates instead of the Council Tax. The amount of Council Tax you pay depends on the size and value of your house or flat (dwelling). You must register to pay Council Tax when you move into a new property, either as the owner or the tenant. You can pay the tax in one payment, in two instalments, or in ten instalments (from April to January).

If only one person lives in the flat or house, you get a 25% reduction on your Council Tax. (This does not apply in Northern Ireland). You may also get a reduction if someone in the property has a disability. People on a low income or who receive benefits such as Income Support or Jobseeker's Allowance can get Council Tax Benefit. You can get advice on this from the local authority or the Citizens Advice Bureau.

BUILDINGS AND HOUSEHOLD INSURANCE

If you buy a home with a mortgage, you must insure the building against fire, theft and accidental damage. The landlord should arrange insurance for rented buildings. It is also wise to insure your possessions against theft or damage. There are many companies that provide insurance.

NEIGHBOURS

If you live in rented accommodation, you will have a tenancy agreement. This explains all the conditions of your tenancy. It will probably include

For further information on how to find the best financial product, from mortgages to telephone services, utilities suppliers to household insurance see the monthly magazine, *Which? Money.*

information on what to do if you have problems with your housing. Occasionally, there may be problems with your neighbours. If you do have problems with your neighbours, they can usually be solved by speaking to them first. If you cannot solve the problem, speak to your landlord, local authority or housing association. Keep a record of the problems in case you have to show exactly what the problems are and when they started. Neighbours who cause a very serious nuisance may be taken to court and can be evicted from their home.

There are several mediation organisations which help neighbours to solve their disputes without having to go to court. Mediators talk to both sides and try to find a solution acceptable to both. You can get details of mediation organisations from the local authority, the Citizens Advice Bureau, and Mediation UK on 0117 904 6661 or visit: www.mediationuk.co.uk

Check that you understand
- The process for buying and renting accommodation
- Where to get advice about accommodation and moving
- The role of an estate agent
- Housing priorities for local authorities
- Where to get help if you are homeless
- How you can pay for the water you use at home
- Recycling your waste
- What Council Tax pays for
- What to do if you have problems with your neighbours

Money and credit

This section provides an overview of basic financial arrangements in the UK. These include currency, banking, credit, savings, insurance and social security.

In this section there is information about:
• Money and credit

Bank notes in the UK come in denominations (values) of £5, £10, £20 and £50. Northern Ireland and Scotland have their own bank notes which are valid everywhere in the UK, though sometimes people may not realise this and may not wish to accept them.

THE EURO

In January 2002 twelve European Union (EU) states adopted the euro as their common currency. The UK government decided not to adopt the euro at that time, and has said it will only do so if the British people vote for the euro in a referendum. The euro does circulate to some extent in Northern Ireland, particularly in the towns near the border with Ireland.

FOREIGN CURRENCY

You can get or change foreign currency at banks, building societies, large post offices and exchange shops or bureaux de change. You might have to order some currencies in advance. The exchange rates vary and you should check for the best deal.

BANKS AND BUILDING SOCIETIES

Most adults in the UK have a bank or building society account. Many large national banks or building societies have branches in towns and cities throughout the UK. It is worth checking the different types of account each one offers. Many employers pay salaries directly into a bank or building society account. There are many banks and building societies to choose from. To open an account you need to show documents to prove your identity, such as a passport, immigration document or driving licence. You also need to show something with your address on it like a tenancy agreement or household bill. It is also possible to open bank accounts in some supermarkets or on the internet.

" To open a bank account you need to show documents to prove your identity, such as a passport, immigration document or driving licence. **"**

CASH AND DEBIT CARDS

Cash cards allow you to use cash machines to withdraw money from your account. For this you need a Personal Identification Number (PIN) which you must keep secret. A debit card allows you to pay for things without using cash. You must have enough money in your account to cover what you buy. If you lose your cash card or debit card you must inform the bank immediately.

CREDIT AND STORE CARDS

Credit cards can be used to buy things in shops, on the telephone and over the internet. A store card is like a credit card but used only in a specific shop. Credit and store cards do not draw money from your bank account but you will be sent a bill every month. If you do not pay the total amount on the bill, you are charged interest. Although credit and store cards are useful, the interest is usually very high and many people fall into debt this way. If you lose your credit or store cards you must inform the company immediately.

CREDIT AND LOANS

People in the UK often borrow money from banks and other organisations to pay for things like household goods, cars and holidays. This is more common in the UK than in many other countries. You must be very sure of the terms and conditions when you decide to take out a loan. You can get advice on loans from the Citizens Advice Bureau if you are uncertain.

BEING REFUSED CREDIT

Banks and other organisations use different information about you to make a decision about a loan, such as your occupation, address, salary and previous credit record. If you apply for a loan you might be refused. If this happens, you have the right to ask the reason why.

CREDIT UNIONS

Credit unions are financial co-operatives owned and controlled by their members. The members pool their savings and then make loans from this pool. Interest rates in credit unions are usually lower than banks and building societies. There are credit unions in many cities and towns. To find the nearest credit union contact the Association of British Credit Unions (ABCUL) on: www.abcul.coop

INSURANCE

As well as insuring their property and possessions, many people insure their credit cards and mobile phones. They also buy insurance when they travel abroad in case they lose their luggage or need medical treatment. Insurance is compulsory if you have a car or motorcycle. You can usually arrange insurance directly with an insurance company, or you can use a broker who will help you get the best deal.

SOCIAL SECURITY

The UK has a system of social security which pays welfare benefits to people who do not have enough money to live on. Benefits are usually available for the sick and disabled, older people, the unemployed and those on low incomes. People who do not have legal rights of residence (or 'settlement') in the UK cannot usually receive benefits. Arrangements for paying and receiving benefits are complex because they have to cover people in many different situations. Guides to benefits are available from Jobcentre Plus offices, local libraries, post offices and the Citizens Advice Bureau.

Check that you understand
- What you need to open a bank or building society account
- What debit, credit and store cards are
- What a credit union is
- What insurance is
- How to get help with benefits and problems with debt

Health

Through the National Health Service (NHS), UK residents enjoy access to free healthcare. This section outlines what that care comprises and what areas of healthcare you will be charged for.

In this section there is information about:
- Health
- Pregnancy and care of young children

Healthcare in the UK is organised under the National Health Service (NHS). The NHS began in 1948, and is one of the largest organisations in Europe. It provides all residents with free healthcare and treatment.

FINDING A DOCTOR

Family doctors are called General Practitioners (GPs) and they work in surgeries. GPs often work together in a group practice. This is sometimes called a Primary Health Care Centre.

Your GP is responsible for organising the health treatment you receive. Treatment can be for physical and mental illnesses. If you need to see a specialist, you must go to your GP first. Your GP will then refer you to a specialist in a hospital. Your GP can also refer you for specialist treatment if you have special needs.

" The NHS began in 1948, and is one of the largest organisations in Europe. It provides all residents with free healthcare and treatment. "

You can get a list of local GPs from libraries, post offices, the tourist information office, the Citizens Advice Bureau, the local Health Authority and from the following websites:

- www.nhs.uk/ for health practitioners in England
- www.wales.nhs.uk/directory.cfm for health practitioners in Wales
- www.n-i.nhs.uk for health practitioners in Northern Ireland

- www.show.scot.nhs.uk/findnearest/healthservices in Scotland
- You can also ask neighbours and friends for the name of their local doctor.

You can attend a hospital without a GP's letter only in the case of an emergency. If you have an emergency you should go to the Accident and Emergency (A & E) department of the nearest hospital.

REGISTERING WITH A GP

You should look for a GP as soon as you move to a new area. You should not wait until you are ill. The health centre, or surgery, will tell you what you need to do to register. Usually you must have a medical card. If you do not have one, the GP's receptionist should give you a form to send to the local health authority. They will then send you a medical card.

Before you register you should check the surgery can offer what you need. For example, you might need a woman GP or maternity services. Sometimes GPs have many patients and are unable to accept new ones. If you cannot find a GP, you can ask your local health authority to help you find one.

❝ Everything you tell the GP is completely confidential and cannot be passed on to anyone else without your permission. ❞

USING YOUR DOCTOR

All patients registering with a GP are entitled to a free health check. Appointments to see the GP can be made by phone or in person. Sometimes you might have to wait several days before you can see a doctor. If you need immediate medical attention ask for an urgent appointment. You should go to the GP's surgery a few minutes before the appointment. If you cannot attend or do not need the appointment any more, you must let the surgery know. The GP needs patients to answer all questions as fully as possible in order to find out what is wrong. Everything you tell the GP is completely confidential and cannot be passed on to anyone else without your permission. If you do not understand something, ask for clarification. If you have difficulties with English, bring someone who can help you, or ask the receptionist for an interpreter. This must be done when you make the appointment. If you have asked for an interpreter, it is important that you keep your appointment because this service is expensive.

In exceptional circumstances, GPs can visit patients at home but they always give priority to people who are unable to travel. If you call the GP outside normal working hours, you will have to answer several questions about your situation. This is to assess how serious your case is. You will then be told if a doctor can come to your home. You might be advised to go to the nearest A&E department.

CHARGES

Treatment from the GP is free but you have to pay a charge for your medicines and for certain services, such as vaccinations for travel abroad. If the GP decides you need to take medicine you will be given a prescription. You must take this to a pharmacy (chemist).

PRESCRIPTIONS

Prescriptions are free for anyone who is

- Under 16 years of age (under 25 in Wales)
- Under 19 and in full-time education
- Aged 60 or over
- Pregnant or with a baby under 12 months old
- Suffering from a specified medical condition
- Receiving Income Support; Jobseekers' Allowance, Working Families or Disabilities Tax Credit.

FEELING UNWELL

If you or your child feels unwell you have the following options:

For information or advice

- Ask your local pharmacist (chemist). The pharmacy can give advice on medicines and some illnesses and conditions that are not serious
- Speak to a nurse by phoning NHS Direct on 0845 46 47
- Use the NHS Direct website, NHS Direct Online: www.nhsdirect.nhs.uk

To see a doctor or nurse

- Make an appointment to see your GP or a nurse working in the surgery
- Visit an NHS walk-in centre.

For urgent medical treatment

- Contact your GP
- Go to your nearest hospital with an Accident and Emergency department
- Call 999 for an ambulance. Calls are free. ONLY use this service for a real emergency.

NHS Direct is a 24-hour telephone service which provides information on particular health conditions. Telephone: 0845 46 47. You may ask for an interpreter for advice in your own language. In Scotland, contact NHS24 at: www.nhs24.com telephone 08454 24 24 24.

NHS Direct Online is a website providing information about health services and several medical conditions and treatments: www.nhsdirect.nhs.uk

NHS walk-in centres provide treatment for minor injuries and illnesses seven days a week. You do not need an appointment. For details of your nearest centre call NHS Direct or visit the NHS website at: www.nhs.uk (for Northern Ireland www.n-i.nhs.uk) and click on 'local NHS services'.

GOING INTO HOSPITAL

If you need minor tests at a hospital, you will probably attend the Outpatients department. If your treatment takes several hours, you will go into hospital as a day patient. If you need to stay overnight, you will go into hospital as an in-patient.

You should take personal belongings with you, such as a towel, night clothes, things for washing, and a dressing gown. You will receive all your meals while you are an in-patient. If you need advice about going into hospital, contact Customer Services or the Patient Advice and Liaison Service (PALS) at the hospital where you will receive treatment.

 From 1 April 2007, the NHS prescription charge was abolished for people in Wales. This means that if you live in Wales, you no longer need to pay for medicines prescribed for you by a doctor. However, for the purposes of the current Life in the UK Test you will be asked questions on the official Home Office text, which was published before the Welsh prescription charges were abolished.

DENTISTS

You can get the name of a dentist by asking at the local library, at the Citizens Advice Bureau and through NHS Direct. Most people have to pay for dental treatment. Some dentists work for the NHS and some are private. NHS dentists charge less than private dentists, but some dentists have two sets of charges, both NHS and private. A dentist should explain your treatment and the charges before the treatment begins.

Free dental treatment is available to

- People under 18 (in Wales people under 25 and over 60)
- Pregnant women and women with babies under 12 months old
- People on income support, Jobseekers' Allowance or Pension Credit Guarantee.

OPTICIANS

Most people have to pay for sight tests and glasses, except children, people over 60, people with certain eye conditions and people receiving certain benefits. In Scotland, eye tests are free.

PREGNANCY AND CARE OF YOUNG CHILDREN

If you are pregnant you will receive regular ante-natal care. This is available from your local hospital, local health centre or from special antenatal clinics. You will receive support from a GP and from a midwife. Midwives work in hospitals or health centres. Some GPs do not provide maternity services so you may wish to look for another GP during your pregnancy. In the UK women usually have their babies in hospital, especially if it is their first baby. It is common for the father to attend the birth, but only if the mother wants him to be there.

A short time after you have your child, you will begin regular contact with a health visitor. She or he is a qualified nurse and can advise you about caring for your baby. The first visits will be in your home, but after that you might meet the health visitor at a clinic. You can ask advice from your health visitor until your child is five years old. In most towns and cities there are mother and toddler groups or playgroups for small children. These

 All children from the age of three are entitled to some free early years education in a nursery school or similar. For further information see www.surestart.gov.uk or call 0870 000 22 88.

often take place at local churches and community centres. You might be able to send your child to a nursery school (see Going to school on page 94).

INFORMATION ON PREGNANCY

You can get information on maternity and ante-natal services in your area from your local health authority, a health visitor or your GP. The number of your health authority will be in the phone book.

The Family Planning Association (FPA) gives advice on contraception and sexual health. The FPA helpline is 0845 310 1334, or: www.fpa.org.uk

The National Childbirth Trust gives information and support in pregnancy, childbirth and early parenthood: www.nctpregnancyandbabycare.com

If your child is born in Scotland, you will need to register his or her birth with the Registrar of Births, Deaths and Marriages within 21 days. For the purposes of the Life in the UK Test, you will need to learn the official text which does not mention this fact about registering a birth in Scotland.

REGISTERING A BIRTH

Your must register your baby with the Registrar of Births, Marriages and Deaths (Register Office) within six weeks of the birth. The address of your local Register Office is in the phone book. If the parents are married, either the mother or father can register the birth. If they are not married, only the mother can register the birth. If the parents are not married but want both names on the child's birth certificate, both mother and father must be present when they register their baby.

Check that you understand
- How to find and register with a GP
- What to do if you feel unwell
- How to find other services such as dentists and opticians
- When it is possible to attend A&E without a doctor's letter
- Who can get free prescriptions
- When you should phone 999 or 112
- What NHS Direct can do
- Who can give health advice and treatment when you are pregnant and after you have a baby
- How to register a birth

Everyday needs

Education

Every child in the UK can be educated for free. However, there are also private schools where a fee is charged. This section explores the options open to parents today and provides an insight into adult education and universities.

In this section there is information about:
- Education

GOING TO SCHOOL

Education in the UK is free and compulsory for all children between the ages of 5 and 16 (4 to 16 in Northern Ireland). The education system varies in England, Scotland, Wales and Northern Ireland.

The child's parent or guardian is responsible for making sure their child goes to school, arrives on time and attends for the whole school year. If they do not do this, the parent or guardian may be prosecuted.

Some areas of the country offer free nursery education for children over the age of 3. In most parts of the UK, compulsory education is divided into two stages, primary and secondary. In some places there is a middle-school system. In England and Wales the primary stage lasts from 5 to 11, in Scotland from 5 to 12 and in Northern Ireland from 4 to 11. The secondary stage lasts until the age of 16. At that age young people can choose to leave school or to continue with their education until they are 17 or 18.

Details of local schools are available from your local education authority office or website. The addresses and phone numbers of local education authorities are in the phone book.

For children starting secondary school from September 2008, the minimum leaving age will be 17. These children will turn 17 in 2014 and 2015. For the purposes of the current Life in the UK Test, which is based on the official Home Office text printed here, children must attend school between the ages of 5 and 16.

PRIMARY SCHOOLS
These are usually schools where both boys and girls learn together and are usually close to a child's home. Children tend to be with the same group and teacher all day. Schools encourage parents to help their children with learning, particularly with reading and writing.

❝ Secondary schools are larger than primary schools. Most are mixed sex, although there are single sex schools in some areas. ❞

SECONDARY SCHOOLS
At age 11 (12 in Scotland) children go to secondary school. This might normally be the school nearest their home, but parents in England and Wales are allowed to express a preference for a different school. In some areas, getting a secondary school place in a preferred school can be difficult, and parents often apply to several schools in order to make sure their child gets offered a place. In Northern Ireland many schools select children through a test taken at the age of 11.

If the preferred school has enough places, the child will be offered a place. If there are not enough places, children will be offered places according to the school's admission arrangements. Admission arrangements vary from area to area.

Secondary schools are larger than primary schools. Most are mixed sex, although there are single sex schools in some areas. Your local education authority will give you information on schools in your area. It will also tell you which schools have spaces and give you information about why some children will be given places when only a few are available and why other children might not. It will also tell you how to apply for a secondary school place.

COSTS
Education at state schools in the UK is free, but parents have to pay for school uniforms and sportswear. There are sometimes extra charges for music lessons and for school outings. Parents on low incomes can get help with costs, and with the cost of school meals. You can get advice on this from the local education authority or the Citizens Advice Bureau.

CHURCH AND OTHER FAITH SCHOOLS
Some primary and secondary schools in the UK are linked to the Church of England or the Roman Catholic Church. These are called 'faith schools'. In some areas there are

Muslim, Jewish and Sikh schools. In Northern Ireland, some schools are called Integrated Schools. These schools aim to bring children of different religions together. Information on faith schools is available from your local education authority.

INDEPENDENT SCHOOLS

Independent schools are private schools. They are not run or paid for by the state. Independent secondary schools are also sometimes called public schools. There are about 2,500 independent schools in the UK. About 8% of children go to these schools. At independent schools parents must pay the full cost of their child's education. Some independent schools offer scholarships which pay some or all of the costs of the child's education.

THE SCHOOL CURRICULUM

All state, primary and secondary schools in England, Wales and Northern Ireland follow the National Curriculum. This covers English, maths, science, design and technology, information and communication technology (ICT), history, geography, modern foreign languages, art and design, music, physical education (PE) and citizenship. In Wales, children learn Welsh.

In some primary schools in Wales, all the lessons are taught in Welsh. In Scotland, pupils follow a broad curriculum informed by national guidance. Schools must, by law, provide religious education (RE) to all pupils. Parents are allowed to withdraw their children from these lessons. RE lessons have a Christian basis but children also learn about the other major religions.

❝ All state, primary and secondary schools in England, Wales and Northern Ireland follow the National Curriculum. In Scotland, pupils follow a broad curriculum informed by national guidance. ❞

ASSESSMENT

In England, the curriculum is divided into four stages, called Key Stages. After each stage children are tested. They take Key Stage tests (also called SATs) at ages 7, 11 and 14. At 16 they usually take the General Certificates of Secondary Education (GCSEs) in several subjects, although some schools also offer other qualifications. At 18, young people who have stayed at school do AGCEs (Advanced GCE levels) often just called A levels.

Study tip: Work through a mind blank

One of the greatest fears we all have in a test situation is a blank mind. If this happens to you, don't just sit there staring at the same question, leave it and move on to the questions you do know the answers to. Once you have completed them, you can go back to the ones you are stuck on. Chances are you will have relaxed by then and will be able to answer these too. If not, jot some notes down on a piece of paper. The word association may help to jog your memory.

In Wales, schools follow the Welsh National Curriculum but have abolished national tests for children at age 7 and 11. There are also plans in Wales to stop testing children at 14. Teachers in Wales still have to assess and report on their pupils' progress and achievements at 7 and 11.

In Scotland, the curriculum is divided into two phases. The first phase is from 5 to 14. There are six levels in this phase, levels A to F. There are no tests for whole groups during this time. Teachers test individual children when they are ready. From 14 to 16, young people do Standard Grade. After 16 they can study at Intermediate, Higher or Advanced level. In Scotland there will soon be a single curriculum for all pupils from age 3 to age 18. This is called A Curriculum for Excellence. More information can be found at www.acurriculumforexcellencescotland.gov.uk.

HELP WITH ENGLISH

If your child's main language is not English, the school may arrange for extra language support from an EAL (English Additional Language) specialist teacher.

CAREERS EDUCATION

All children get careers advice from the age of 14. Advice is also available from Connexions, a national service for young people: telephone 080 800 13219 or: www.connexions-direct.com in England. In Wales, Careers Wales offers advice to children from the age of 11. For further information visit: www.careerswales.com or telephone 0800 100 900.

In Scotland, Careers Scotland provides information, services and support to all ages and stages. For further information visit www.careers-scotland.org.uk or telephone 08458 502 502.

PARENTS AND SCHOOLS

Many parents are involved with their child's school. A number of places on a school's governing body are reserved for parents. The governing body decides how the school is run and administered and produces reports on the progress of the school from year to year. In Scotland, parents can be members of school boards or parent councils.

Schools must be open 190 days a year. Term dates are decided by the governing body or by the local education authority. Children must attend the whole school year. Schools expect parents and guardians to inform them if their child is going to be absent from school. All schools ask parents to sign a home-school agreement. This is a list of things that both the school and the parent or guardian agree to do to ensure a good education for the child. All parents receive a report every year on their child's progress. They also have the chance to go to the school to talk to their child's teachers.

" The governing body decides how a school is run and administered and produces reports on the progress of the school from year to year. "

FURTHER EDUCATION AND ADULT EDUCATION

At 16, young people can leave school or stay on to do A levels (Higher grades in Scotland) in preparation for university. Some young people go to their local further education (FE) college to improve their exam grades or to get new qualifications for a career. Most courses are free up to the age of 19. Young people from families with low incomes can get financial help with their studies when they leave school at 16. This is called the Education Maintenance Allowance (EMA). Information about this is available at your local college or at: www.dfes.gov.uk.

Further education colleges also offer courses to adults over the age of 18. These include courses for people wishing to improve their skills in English. These courses are called ESOL (English for Speakers of Other Languages). There are also courses for English speakers who need to improve their literacy and numeracy and for people who need to learn new

For further information on English courses for speakers of other languages, as well as literacy and numeracy courses for adults, contact your local college or library or see www.learndirect.co.uk

skills for employment. ESOL courses are also available in community centres and training centres. There is sometimes a waiting list for ESOL courses because demand is high. In England and Wales, ESOL literacy and numeracy courses are also called Skills for Life courses. You can get information at your local college or local library or from Learndirect on 0800 100 900.

Many people join other adult education classes to learn a new skill or hobby and to meet new people. Classes are very varied and range from sports to learning a musical instrument or a new language. Details are usually available from your local library, college or adult education centre.

UNIVERSITY

More young people go to university now than in the past. Many go after A levels (or Higher grades in Scotland) at age 18 but it is also possible to go to university later in life. At present, most students in England, Wales and Northern Ireland have to pay towards the cost of their tuition fees and to pay for their living expenses. In Scotland there are no tuition fees but after students finish university they pay back some of the cost of their education in a payment called an endowment. At present, universities can charge up to £3,000 per year for their tuition fees, but students do not have to pay anything towards their fees before or during their studies. The government pays their tuition fees and then charges for them when a student starts working after university. Some families on low incomes receive help with their children's tuition fees. This is called a grant. The universities also give help, in the form of bursaries. Most students get a low-interest student loan from a bank. This pays for their living costs while they are at university. When a student finishes university and starts working, he or she must pay back the loan.

Check that you understand
- The different stages of a child's education
- That there are differences in the education systems in England, Scotland, Wales and Northern Ireland
- That there are different kinds of school, and that some of them charge fees
- What the National Curriculum is
- What the governing body of a school does
- Options for young people at the age of 16
- Courses available at FE colleges
- Where you can get English classes or other education for adults, including university

Leisure

This section provides information on things to do and see in the UK during your spare time. It explains film classifications, outlines the legal requirement for a television licence and mentions clubs, places of interest, pubs and gambling. It also outlines how animal welfare is protected by law.

In this section there is information about:
• Leisure

INFORMATION

Information about theatre, cinema, music and exhibitions is found in local newspapers, local libraries and tourist information offices. Many museums and art galleries are free.

FILM, VIDEO AND DVD

Films in the UK have a system to show if they are suitable for children. This is called the classification system. If a child is below the age of the classification, they should not watch the film at a cinema or on DVD. All films receive a classification, as follows:

U (Universal): suitable for anyone aged 4 years and over.
PG (parental guidance): suitable for everyone but some parts of the film might be unsuitable for children. Their parents should decide.
12 or 12a: children under 12 are not allowed to see or rent the film unless they are with an adult.
15: children under 15 are not allowed to see or rent the film.
18: no one under 18 is allowed to see or rent the film.
R18: no one under 18 is allowed to see the film, which is only available in specially licensed cinemas.

For information on attractions and events, both in your area and nationwide, see the website of Britain's official tourism agency, Visit Britain, www.visitbritain.co.uk

TELEVISION AND RADIO

Anyone in the UK with a television (TV), DVD or video recorder, computer or any device which is used for watching or recording TV programmes must be covered by a valid television licence. One licence covers all of the equipment at one address, but people who rent different rooms in a shared house must each buy a separate licence.

A colour TV licence currently costs £131.50 (2006) and lasts for 12 months. People aged 75 or over can apply for a free TV licence. Blind people can claim a 50% discount on their TV licence. You risk prosecution and a fine if you watch TV but are not covered by a TV licence. There are many ways to buy a TV licence including from local Pay Point outlets or on-line at: www.tvlicensing.co.uk. It is also possible to pay for the licence in instalments. For more information telephone 0870 576 3763 or write to TV Licensing, Bristol BS98 1TL.

❝ Anyone in the UK with a television (TV), DVD or video recorder, computer or any device which is used for watching or recording TV programmes must be covered by a valid television licence. ❞

SPORTS, CLUBS AND SOCIETIES

Information about local clubs and societies can usually be found at local libraries or through your local authority. For information about sports you should ask in the local leisure centre. Libraries and leisure centres often organise activities for children during the school holidays.

PLACES OF INTEREST

The UK has a large network of public footpaths in the countryside. Many parts of the countryside and places of interest are kept open by the National Trust. This is a charity that works to preserve important buildings and countryside in the UK. Information about National Trust buildings and areas open to the public is available on: www.nationaltrust.org.uk

PUBS AND NIGHT CLUBS

Public houses, or pubs, are an important part of social life in the UK. To drink alcohol in a pub you must be 18 or over. People under 18 are not allowed to buy alcohol in a supermarket or in an off-licence either.

Everyday needs

The landlord of the pub may allow people of 14 to come into the pub but they are not allowed to drink. At 16, people can drink wine or beer with a meal in a hotel or restaurant.

Pubs are usually open during the day and until 11 p.m. If a pub wants to stay open later, it must apply for a special licence. Night clubs open and close later than pubs.

❝ Public houses, or pubs, are an important part of social life in the UK. To drink alcohol in a pub you must be 18 or over. ❞

BETTING AND GAMBLING

People under 18 are not allowed into betting shops or gambling clubs. There is a National Lottery for which draws, with large prizes, are made every week. You can enter by buying a ticket or a scratch card. People under 16 are not allowed to buy a lottery ticket or scratch card.

PETS

Many people in the UK have pets such as cats and dogs. It is against the law to treat a pet cruelly or to neglect it. All dogs in public places must wear a collar showing the name and address of the owner. The owner is responsible for keeping the dog under control and for cleaning up after the animal in a public place. Vaccinations and medical treatment for animals are available from veterinary surgeons (vets). If you cannot afford to pay a vet, you can go to a charity called the PDSA (People's Dispensary for Sick Animals). To find your nearest branch, visit: www.pdsa.org.uk

 In addition to the National Trust, English Heritage is a charity that works to protect and promote Britain's historic environment. For further details see, www.english-heritage.org.uk

Travel and transport

The majority of journeys throughout the UK are taken by road or rail. This section includes how to buy rail tickets, how to obtain a driving licence and what laws apply to driving in the UK.

In this section there is information about:
● Travel and transport

TRAINS, BUSES AND COACHES

For information about trains telephone the National Rail Enquiry Service:
08457 48 49 50 or visit: www.nationalrail.co.uk
For trains in Northern Ireland, phone Translink on 028 90 66 66 30
or visit: www.translink.co.uk
For information about local bus times phone 0870 608 250.
For information on coaches, telephone National Express on
08705 80 80 80, or visit: www.nationalexpress.com
For coaches in Scotland, telephone Scottish Citylink
on 08705 50 50 50 or visit www.citylink.co.uk
For Northern Ireland, visit: www.translink.co.uk

Usually, tickets for trains and underground systems such as the London Underground must be bought before you get on the train. The fare varies according to the day and time you wish to travel. Travelling in the rush hour is always more expensive. Discount tickets are available for families, people aged 60 and over, disabled people, students and people under 26. Ask at your local train station for details. Failure to buy a ticket may result in a penalty.

TAXIS

To operate legally, all taxis and minicabs must be licensed and display a licence plate. Taxis and cabs with no licence are not insured for fare-paying passengers and are not always safe. Women should not use unlicensed minicabs.

DRIVING

You must be at least 17 to drive a car or motorcycle, 18 to drive a medium-sized lorry, and 21 to drive a large lorry or bus. To drive a lorry, minibus or bus with more than eight passenger seats, you must have a special licence.

❝ If your driving licence is from a country in the European Union (EU), Iceland, Liechtenstein or Norway, you can drive in the UK for as long as your licence is valid. ❞

THE DRIVING LICENCE

You must have a driving licence to drive on public roads. To get a driving licence you must pass a test. There are many driving schools where you can learn with the help of a qualified instructor.

You get a full driving licence in three stages:

1 Apply for a provisional licence. You need this licence while you are learning to drive. With this you are allowed to drive a motorcycle up to 125cc or a car. You must put L plates on the vehicle, or D plates in Wales. Learner drivers cannot drive on a motorway. If you drive a car, you must be with someone who is over 21 and who has had a full licence for over three years. You can get an application form for a provisional licence from a post office.

2 Pass a written theory test.

3 Pass a practical driving test.

Drivers may use their licence until they are 70. After that the licence is valid for three years at a time.

In Northern Ireland, a newly-qualified driver must display an R-Plate (for registered driver) for one year after passing the test.

 For further information on how to apply for any kind of driving licence, contact the Driver and Vehicle Licensing Agency (DVLA). Tel: 0870 240 0009 Website: www.dvla.gov.uk

OVERSEAS LICENCES

If your driving licence is from a country in the European Union (EU), Iceland, Liechtenstein or Norway, you can drive in the UK for as long as your licence is valid.

If you have a licence from a country outside the EU, you may use it in the UK for up to 12 months. During this time you must get a UK provisional driving licence and pass both the UK theory and practical driving tests, or you will not be able to drive after 12 months.

INSURANCE

It is a criminal offence to have a car without proper motor insurance. Drivers without insurance can receive very high fines. It is also illegal to allow someone to use your car if they are not insured to drive it.

ROAD TAX AND MOT

You must also pay a tax to drive your car on the roads. This is called road tax. Your vehicle must have a road tax disc which shows you have paid. You can buy this at the post office. If you do not pay the road tax, your vehicle may be clamped or towed away.

If your vehicle is over three years old, you must take it every year for a Ministry of Transport (MOT) test. You can do this at an approved garage. The garage will give you an MOT certificate when your car passes the test. It is an offence not to have an MOT certificate. If you do not have an MOT certificate, your insurance will not be valid.

❝ It is illegal to drive when you are over the alcohol limit or drunk. The police can stop you and give you a test to see how much alcohol you have in your body. ❞

SAFETY

Everyone in a vehicle should wear a seat belt. Children under 12 years of age may need a special booster seat. Motorcyclists and their passengers must wear a crash helmet (this law does not apply to Sikh men if they are wearing a turban). It is illegal to drive while holding a mobile phone.

SPEED LIMITS

For cars and motorcycles the speed limits are:

- 30 miles per hour (mph) in built-up areas, unless a sign shows a different limit
- 60 mph on single carriageways
- 70 mph on motorways and dual carriageways

Speed limits are lower for buses, lorries and cars pulling caravans.

It is illegal to drive when you are over the alcohol limit or drunk. The police can stop you and give you a test to see how much alcohol you have in your body. This is called a breathalyser test. If a driver has more than the permitted amount of alcohol (called being 'over the limit') or refuses to take the test, he or she will be arrested. People who drink and drive can expect to be disqualified from driving for a long period.

ACCIDENTS

If you are involved in a road accident:

- don't drive away without stopping – this is a criminal offence
- call the police and ambulance on 999 or 112 if someone is injured
- get the names, addresses, vehicle registration numbers and insurance details of the other drivers
- give your details to the other drivers or passengers and to the police
- make a note of everything that happened and contact your insurance company as soon as possible.

Note that if you admit the accident was your fault, the insurance company may refuse to pay. It is better to wait until the insurance company decides for itself whose fault the accident was.

 For further information on the Government's plans to introduce ID cards and the latest news concerning any developments in this area, see the website of the Identity and Passport Service: www.ips.gov.uk/identity

Identity documents

At present, UK citizens do not have to carry identity (ID) cards. The government is, however, making plans to introduce them in the next few years.

In this section there is information about:
• Identity documents

PROVING YOUR IDENTITY

You may have to prove your identity at different times, such as when you open a bank account, rent accommodation, enrol for a college course, hire a car, apply for benefits such as housing benefit or apply for a marriage certificate. Different organisations may ask for different documents as proof of identity. These can include:

• Official documents from the Home Office showing your immigration status
• A certificate of identity
• A passport or travel document
• A National Insurance (NI) number card
• A provisional or full driving licence
• A recent gas, electricity or phone bill showing your name and address
• A rent or benefits book.

Check that you understand
• How films are classified
• Why you need a television licence
• The rules about the selling and drinking of alcohol
• How to get a driving licence
• What you need to do to be allowed to drive a vehicle in the UK
• What you should do if you have an accident
• When you might have to prove your identity, and how you can do it

Everyday needs

Practice questions

For the answers to these questions, see page 190.

1 What is a mortgage?
A A special loan from a bank or building society to buy property
B A small two-bedroom property
C Insurance to cover payments on property when you are unemployed
D The tax that is paid when a property is bought or sold

2 What does the amount of council tax you pay depend on?
A The size and value of your property
B How much you earn
C How close you are to the town centre
D The number of windows in your property

3 Who collects household refuse?
A The local authority
B The neighbourhood services agency
C The recycling department
D The landfill authority

4 What is a credit union?
A A financial co-operative owned and controlled by its members
B A company that issues credit cards
C A credit reference agency
D A type of credit card insurance

5 If you are having problems with your landlord where can you go for help and advice? (Select two options)
A A Primary Health Care Centre
B The DVLA
C The housing department of the local authority
D The Citizens Advice Bureau

6 What numbers can you dial for the police, fire or ambulance services?
A 192 or 118
B 999 or 112
C 100 or 150
D 151 or 152

7 True or False? People who have the legal right of residence in the UK can usually receive benefits.
A True
B False

8 In most parts of the UK, compulsory education is divided into what TWO of the following? (Select two options)
A Nursery school
B Primary school
C Secondary school
D College

9 **What is a tenancy agreement?**
A A document that explains the conditions you must follow while renting a property
B A document from your employer confirming that you are working
C A document from the Home Office confirming that you are legally allowed to live in the UK
D A document from your bank confirming that you can pay a deposit

10 **What is another name for local authority housing?**
A Social housing
B Co-operative housing
C Council housing
D Local housing

11 **What is Shelter?**
A A housing charity
B A dog kennel
C A house building company
D A type of umbrella

12 **True or False? The rate of interest on credit and store cards is usually very high.**
A True
B False

13 **Where can you get information about local schools?**
A Your local education authority
B Your nearest school
C Your local MP
D NHS Direct

14 **True or False? Insurance is compulsory if you have a car or motorcycle.**
A True
B False

15 **Who does not have to pay for a sight test? (Select two options)**
A Anyone in Scotland
B Children and people over 60
C People who have always lived in the United Kingdom and who hold a British passport
D Everyone – sight tests are free

16 **True or False? The National Health Service provides all residents with free healthcare and treatment.**
A True
B False

17 **What is a GP?**
A A Group Practice
B A doctor who is a General Practitioner
C A Great Principle
D A Generalised Programme

18 **Who should be present when registering a child's birth if the parents are unmarried and want to be named on the birth certificate?**
A The mother
B The father
C Both parents
D The grandparents

19 **What happens if the parents' preferred secondary school does not have enough places?**
A Children living close to the school are given priority
B Children are offered a place according to the school's admission requirements
C Girls are given priority
D Children with brothers or sisters at the school are given priority

20 Where do you get a medical card?

A From your GP

B From the local health authority

C From the Citizens Advice Bureau

D From the Jobcentre

21 What is a faith school?

A A school that studies all religions

B A school that has no religious studies

C A school linked to a specific religion

D A school that believes in strong discipline

22 In what part of the UK can you find the euro in circulation?

A England

B Wales

C Scotland

D Northern Ireland

23 What is the age requirement for someone wanting to see an '18' classified film?

A Children under 12 are not allowed to see or rent the film unless they are with an adult

B Children under 15 are not allowed to see or rent the film

C No one under 18 is allowed to see or rent the film

D No one under 18 is allowed to see the film, which is only available in specially licensed cinemas

24 How old does someone have to be to apply for a free TV licence?

A 65 or over

B 70 or over

C 75 or over

D 80 or over

25 True or False? Scottish Schools will follow a Curriculum for Excellence.

A True

B False

26 What is the charity called that works to preserve many important buildings and countryside in the UK?

A The Heritage Council

B The National Trust

C The Countryside Commission

D National Heritage

27 What organisation provides careers advice (in England)?

A Careers England

B Connexions

C Career Connections

D Further Careers

28 What is the name of the tax you must pay to drive your car on public roads?

A Drivers' tax

B Road tax

C Car driving tax

D MOT tax

29 Which of these statements is correct?

A In England, Scotland and Northern Ireland learner drivers have to put an L plate on their cars or motorcycles

B In England, Scotland and Northern Ireland learner drivers have to put a D plate on their cars or motorcycles

30 True or False? It is compulsory for everyone in a vehicle to wear a seat belt.

A True

B False

Employment

In the UK there are several laws and organisations designed to help you find a job and stay safe and well while you are working. This chapter provides an insight into these areas, as well as informing you of your employment rights. In addition, it explains how, if you earn an income in the UK, you will be liable to pay income tax and National Insurance.

Looking for work

This section outlines how to go about looking for a job. It includes information about qualifications and training, as well as where to find advice and support on skills and training issues.

In this section there is information about:
- Looking for work and applying for jobs
- Training and volunteering

If you are looking for work, or you are thinking of changing your job, there are a number of ways you can find out about work opportunities. The Home Office provides guidance on who is allowed to work in the UK. Not everyone in the UK is allowed to work and some people need work permits, so it is important to check your status before taking up work. Also, employers have to check that anyone they employ is legally entitled to work in the UK. For more information and guidance, see the Home Office website 'Working in the UK' – www.workingintheuk.gov.uk

Jobs are usually advertised in local and national newspapers, at the local Jobcentre and in employment agencies. You can find the address and telephone number of your local Jobcentre under Jobcentre Plus in the phone book or see: www.jobcentreplus.gov.uk. Some jobs are advertised on supermarket notice boards and in shop windows. These jobs are usually part-time and the wages are often quite low. If there are particular companies you would like to work for, you can look for vacancies on their websites.

Jobcentre Plus is run by a government department – the Department for Work and Pensions. Trained staff give advice and help in finding and applying for jobs as well as claiming benefits. They can also arrange for interpreters. Their website www.jobcentreplus.gov.uk lists vacancies and training opportunities and gives general information on benefits. There is also a low cost telephone service – Jobseeker Direct 0845 60 60 234. This is open 9 a.m. to 6 p.m. on weekdays and 9 a.m. to 1 p.m. on Saturdays.

QUALIFICATIONS

Applicants for some jobs need special training or qualifications. If you have qualifications from another country, you can find out how they compare with qualifications in the UK at the National Academic Recognition Information Centre (NARIC), www.naric.org.uk

For further information contact UK NARIC, ECCTIS Ltd, Oriel House, Oriel Road, Cheltenham Glos, GL50 1XP telephone: 0870 990 4088, email: info@naric.org.uk

APPLICATIONS

Interviews for lower paid and local jobs can often be arranged by telephone or in person. For many jobs you need to fill in an application form or send a copy of your curriculum vitae (CV) with a covering letter or letter of application.

A covering letter is usually a short letter attached to a completed application form, while a letter of application gives more detailed information on why you are applying for the job and why you think you are suitable. Your CV gives specific details on your education, qualifications, previous employment, skills and interests. It is important to type any letters and your CV on a computer or word processor as this improves your chance of being called for an interview.

Employers often ask for the names and addresses of one or two referees. These are people such as your current or previous employer or college tutor. Referees need to know you well and to agree to write a short report or reference on your suitability for the job. Personal friends or members of your family are not normally acceptable as referees.

INTERVIEWS

In job descriptions and interviews, employers should give full details of what the job involves, including the pay, holidays and working conditions. If you need more information about any of these, you can ask questions in the interview. In fact asking some questions in the interview shows you are interested and can improve your chance of getting the job.

When you are applying for a job and during the interview, it is important to be honest about your qualifications and experience. If an employer later finds out that you gave incorrect information, you might lose your job.

For further information and advice on finding and applying for jobs see the Which? Essential Guide *CV and Interview Handbook.*

CRIMINAL RECORD

For some jobs, particularly if the work involves working with children or vulnerable people, the employer will ask for your permission to do a criminal record check. You can get more information on this from the Home Office Criminal Records Bureau (CRB) information line, telephone 0870 90 90 811. In Scotland, contact Disclosure Scotland: www.disclosurescotland.co.uk Helpline: 0870 609 6006.

TRAINING

Taking up training helps people improve their qualifications for work. Some training may be offered at work or you can do courses from home or at your local college. This includes English language training. You can get more information from your local library and college or from websites such as www.worktrain.gov.uk and www.learndirect.co.uk. Learndirect offers a range of online training courses at centres across the country. There are charges for courses but you can do free starter or taster sessions. You can get more information from their free information and advice line: 0800 100 900.

VOLUNTEERING AND WORK EXPERIENCE

Some people do voluntary work and this can be a good way to support your local community and organisations which depend on volunteers. It also provides useful experience that can help with future job applications. Your local library will have information about volunteering opportunities. You can also get information and advice from websites such as: www.do-it.org.uk, www.volunteering.org.uk and www.justdosomething.net

---

Check that you understand
- The Home Office provides guidance on who is entitled to work in the UK
- NARIC can advise on how qualifications from overseas compare with qualifications from the UK
- What CVs are
- Who can be a referee
- What happens if any of the information you have given is untrue
- When you need a CRB check
- Where you can find out about training opportunities and job seeking
- Benefits of volunteering in terms of work experience and community involvement

---

Equal rights and discrimination

Laws protect workers from discrimination and poor treatment. This section outlines what discrimination and sexual harassment are, and how people may get help if they find they are treated in this way.

In this section there is information about:
- Equal rights and discrimination

It is against the law for employers to discriminate against someone at work. This means that a person should not be refused work, training or promotion or treated less favourably because of their:

- Sex
- Nationality, race, colour or ethnic group
- Disability
- Religion
- Sexual orientation
- Age.

In Northern Ireland, the law also bans discrimination on grounds of religious belief or political opinion.

The law also says that men and women who do the same job, or work of equal value, should receive equal pay. Almost all the laws protecting people at work apply equally to people doing part-time or full-time jobs.

There are, however a small number of jobs where discrimination laws do not apply. For example, discrimination is not against the law when the job involves working for someone in their own home.

You can get more information about the law and racial discrimination from the Commission for Racial Equality. The Equal Opportunities Commission can help with sex discrimination issues and the Disability Rights Commission deals with disability issues. Each of these organisations offers advice and information and can, in some cases, support individuals. From October 2007 their functions will be brought together in a new Commission for Equality and Human Rights. You can get more information about the laws protecting people at work from the Citizens Advice Bureau website: www.adviceguide.org.uk

In Northern Ireland, the Equality Commission provides information and advice in respect of all forms of unlawful discrimination.

❝ It is against the law for employers to discriminate against someone at work. The law also says that men and women who do the same job, or work of equal value, should receive equal pay. ❞

The Commission for Racial Equality
St Dunstan's House, 201-211 Borough High Street, London SE1 1GZ
Telephone: 020 7939 000, Fax: 020 7939 0001, www.cre.gov.uk

The Equal Opportunities Commission
Arndale House, Arndale Centre, Manchester M4 3EQ
Telephone: 0845 601 5901, Fax: 0161 8388312, www.eoc.org.uk

The Disability Rights Commission
DRC Helpline, FREEPOST MID02164, Stratford upon Avon CV37 9BR
Telephone: 08457 622 633, Fax: 08457 778 878, www.drc.org.uk

The Equality Commission for Northern Ireland
Equality House, 7-9 Shaftesbury Square, Belfast BT2 7DP
Telephone: 028 90 500600, www.equalityni.org

 The Equality and Human Rights Commission came into force in October 2007. It replaces the previous equality commissions and takes on responsibility for the other aspects of equality including age, sexual orientation and religion or belief, as well as human rights. For the purposes of the current UK citizenship test, you will be asked questions based on this official Home Office text, which was published before the Equality and Human Rights Commission was created.

SEXUAL HARASSMENT

Sexual harassment can take different forms. This includes:

- Indecent remarks
- Comments about the way you look that make you feel uncomfortable or humiliated
- Comments or questions about your sex life
- Inappropriate touching or sexual demands
- Bullying behaviour or being treated in a way that is rude, hostile, degrading or humiliating because of your sex.

Men and women can be victims of sexual harassment at work. If this happens to you, tell a friend, colleague or trade union representative and ask the person harassing you to stop. It is a good idea to keep a written record of what happened, the days and times when it happened and who else may have seen or heard the harassment. If the problem continues, report the person to your employer or trade union. Employers are responsible for the behaviour of their employees while they are at work. They should treat complaints of sexual harassment very seriously and take effective action to deal with the problem. If you are not satisfied with your employer's response, you can ask for advice and support from the Equal Opportunities Commission, your trade union or the Citizens Advice Bureau.

&&Employers should treat complaints of sexual harassment very seriously and take effective action to deal with the problem. ,,

Study tip: Eat

Your brain needs energy to work. If you skip breakfast or lunch before your exam, you might be doing yourself a disservice. It's also a good idea to avoid foods with high sugar or fat content, as these may make you feel tired or sluggish.

At work

All workers and employers have responsibilities in the workplace.
For example, employers are legally obliged to pay their staff.
Here is an overview of the issues and obligations concerning work.

In this section there is information about:
- Rights and responsibilities at work

Both employers and employees have legal responsibilities at work.
Employers have to pay employees for the work that they do, treat them
fairly and take responsible care for their health and safety. Employees
should do their work with reasonable skill and care and follow all reasonable
instructions. They should not damage their employer's business.

A WRITTEN CONTRACT OR STATEMENT
Within two months of starting a new job, your employer should give you
a written contract or statement with all the details and conditions for your
work. This should include your responsibilities, pay, working hours, holidays,
sick pay and pension. It should also include the period of notice that both
you and your employer should give for the employment to end. The
contract or written statement is an important document and is very useful
if there is ever a disagreement about your work, pay or conditions.

PAY, HOURS AND HOLIDAYS
Your pay is agreed between you and your employer. There is a minimum
wage in the UK that is a legal right for every employed person above
compulsory school leaving age. The compulsory school leaving age is 16,
but the time in the school year when 16-year-olds can leave school in
England and Wales is different from that in Scotland and Northern Ireland.

 The national minimum wage rates are reviewed and normally increased in
October every year. This official Home Office text, taken from the book,
Life in the United Kingdom: A Journey to Citizenship, gives the rates for the
year following October 2006.

There are different minimum wage rates for different age groups. From October 2006 the rates are as follows:

- For workers aged 22 and above £5.35 an hour
- For 18-21 year olds – £4.45 an hour
- For 16-17 year olds – £3.30 an hour.

Employers who pay their workers less than this are breaking the law. You can get more information from the Central Office of Information Directgov website, www.direct.gov.uk which has a wide range of public service information. Alternatively, you can telephone the National Minimum Wage Helpline, telephone: 0845 600 0678.

Your contract or statement will show the number of hours you are expected to work. Your employer might ask you if you can work more hours than this and it is your decision whether or not you do. Your employer cannot require you to work more hours than the hours agreed on your contract.

If you need to be absent from work, for example if you are ill or you have a medical appointment it is important to tell your employer as soon as you can in advance. Most employees who are 16 or over are entitled to at least four weeks, paid holiday every year. This includes time for national holidays (see Chapter 3). Your employer must give you a pay slip, or a similar written statement, each time you are paid. This must show exactly how much money has been taken off for tax and National Insurance contributions.

Study tip: Sleep

People who are sleep deprived can be more prone to making mistakes. Try to get a good night's sleep before the test and wake up feeling refreshed and raring to go. If you feel refreshed it will also help enhance your positive feelings, which will help you greatly if you are feeling a little stressed or nervous about the test.

TAX

For most people, tax is automatically taken from their earnings by the employer and paid directly to HM Revenue and Customs, the government department responsible for collecting taxes. If you are self-employed, you need to pay your own tax (see page 124). Money raised from income tax pays for government services such as roads, education, police and the armed forces. Occasionally HM Revenue and Customs sends out tax return forms which ask for full financial details. If you receive one, it is important to complete it and return the form as soon as possible. You can get help and advice from the HM Revenue and Customs self-assessment helpline, on: 0845 300 45 55.

" For most people, tax is automatically taken from their earnings by the employer and paid directly to HM Revenue and Customs, the government department responsible for collecting taxes. "

NATIONAL INSURANCE

Almost everybody in the UK who is in paid work, including self-employed people, must pay National Insurance (NI) contributions. Money raised from NI contributions is used to pay contributory benefits such as the State Retirement Pension and helps fund the National Health Service. Employees have their NI contributions deducted from their pay by their employer every week or month. People who are self-employed need to pay NI contributions themselves: Class 2 contributions, either by direct debit or every three months and Class 4 contributions on the profits from their trade or business. Class 4 contributions are paid alongside their income tax. Anyone who does not pay enough NI contributions will not be able to receive certain benefits, such as Jobseeker's Allowance or Maternity Pay, and may not receive a full state retirement pension.

GETTING A NATIONAL INSURANCE NUMBER

Just before their 16th birthday, all young people in the UK are sent a National Insurance number. This is a unique number for each person and it tracks their National Insurance contributions.

Refugees whose asylum applications have been successful have the same rights to work as any other UK citizen and to receive a National Insurance number. People who have applied for asylum and have not received a positive decision do not usually have permission to work and so do not get a National Insurance number.

You need a National Insurance number when you start work. If you do not have a National Insurance number, you can apply for one through Jobcentre Plus or your local Social Security Office. It is a good idea to make an appointment by telephone and ask which documents you need to take with you. You usually need to show your birth certificate, passport and Home Office documents allowing you to stay in the country. If you need information about registering for a National Insurance number, you can telephone the National Insurance Registrations Helpline on 0845 91 57006 or 0845 91 55670.

PENSIONS

Everyone in the UK who has paid enough National Insurance contributions will get a State Pension when they retire. The State Pension age for men is currently 65 years of age and for women it is 60, but the State Pension age for women will increase to 65 in stages between 2010 and 2020. You can find full details of the State Pension scheme on the State Pension website, www.thepensionservice.gov.uk or you can phone the Pension Service Helpline: 0845 606 0265.

In addition to a State Pension, many people also receive a pension through their work and some also pay into a personal pension plan too. It is very important to get good advice about pensions. The Pensions Advisory Service gives free and confidential advice on occupational and personal pensions. Their helpline telephone number is 0845 601 2923 and their website address is www.opas.org.uk. Independent financial advisers can also give advice but you usually have to pay a fee for this service. You can find local financial advisers in the *Yellow Pages* and *Thomson* local guides or on the internet at www.unbiased.co.uk

HEALTH AND SAFETY

Employers have a legal duty to make sure the workplace is safe. Employees also have a legal duty to follow safety regulations and to work safely and responsibly. If you are worried about health and safety at your workplace, talk to your supervisor, manager or trade union representative. You need to follow the right procedures and your employer must not dismiss you or treat you unfairly for raising a concern.

Study tip: Exercise

A great stress buster is exercise. Positive feelings can be induced by exercise through the release of hormones such as serotonin. Exercise can also be an excellent way of taking a break from studying and can give your brain chance to digest and retain the information you have been revising.

TRADE UNIONS

Trade unions are organisations that aim to improve the pay and working conditions of their members. They also give their members advice and support on problems at work. You can choose whether to join a trade union or not and your employer cannot dismiss you or treat you unfairly for being a union member.

You can find details of trade unions in the UK, the benefits they offer to members and useful information on rights at work on the Trades Union Congress (TUC) website, www.tuc.org.uk

PROBLEMS AT WORK

If you have problems of any kind at work, speak to your supervisor, manager, trade union representative or someone else with responsibility as soon as possible. If you need to take any action, it is a good idea to get advice first. If you are a member of a trade union, your representative will help. You can also contact your local Citizens Advice Bureau (CAB) or Law Centre. The national Advisory, Conciliation and Arbitration Service (ACAS) website, www.acas.org.uk gives information on your rights at work. ACAS also offers a national helpline, telephone: 08457 47 47 47.

LOSING YOUR JOB AND UNFAIR DISMISSAL

An employee can be dismissed immediately for serious misconduct at work. Anyone who cannot do their job properly, or is unacceptably late or absent from work, should be given a warning by their employer. If their work, punctuality or attendance does not improve, the employer can give them notice to leave their job.

It is against the law for employers to dismiss someone from work unfairly. If this happens to you, or life at work is made so difficult that you feel you have to leave, you may be able to get compensation if you take your case to an Employment Tribunal. This is a court which specialises in employment matters. You normally only have three months to make a complaint.

If you are dismissed from your job, it is important to get advice on your case as soon as possible. You can ask for advice and information on your legal rights and the best action to take from your trade union representative, a solicitor, a Law Centre or the Citizens Advice Bureau.

REDUNDANCY

If you lose your job because the company you work for no longer needs someone to do your job, or cannot afford to employ you, you may be entitled to redundancy pay. The amount of money you receive depends on the length of time you have been employed. Again your trade union representative, a solicitor, a Law Centre or the Citizens Advice Bureau can advise you.

UNEMPLOYMENT

Most people who become unemployed can claim Jobseeker's Allowance (JSA). This is currently available for men aged 18-65 and women aged 18-60 who are capable of working, available for work and trying to find work. Unemployed 16 and 17-year-olds may not be eligible for Jobseeker's Allowance but may be able to claim a Young Person's Bridging Allowance (YPBA) instead. The local Jobcentre Plus can help with claims. You can get further information from the Citizens Advice Bureau and the Jobcentre Plus website: www.jobcentreplus.gov.uk

❝ Work-based learning programmes offer training to people while they are at work. People receive a wage or allowance and can attend college for one day a week to get a new qualification. ❞

NEW DEAL

New Deal is a government programme that aims to give unemployed people the help and support they need to get into work. Young people who have been unemployed for 6 months and adults who have been unemployed for 18 months are usually required to join New Deal if they wish to continue receiving benefit. There are different New Deal schemes for different age groups. You can find out more about New Deal on 0845 606 2626 or: www.newdeal.gov.uk

The government also runs work-based learning programmes which offer training to people while they are at work. People receive a wage or an allowance and can attend college for one day a week to get a new qualification.

You can find out more about the different government schemes, and the schemes in your area, from Jobcentre Plus, www.jobcentreplus.gov.uk, or your local Citizens Advice Bureau.

Working for yourself

There are approximately 4 million self-employed people working in the UK. All of them have to pay income tax and National Insurance. This section details your rights and responsibilities if you are self-employed, plus where you can find help and advice to set up and run your own business.

In this section there is information about:
• Working for yourself

TAX

Self-employed people are responsible for paying their own tax and National Insurance. They have to keep detailed records of what they earn and spend on the business and send their business accounts to HM Revenue and Customs every year. Most self-employed people use an accountant to make sure they pay the correct tax and claim all the possible tax allowances.

As soon as you become self-employed you should register yourself for tax and National Insurance by ringing the HM Revenue and Customs telephone helpline for people who are self-employed, on 0845 915 4515.

❝ Self-employed people are responsible for paying their own tax and National Insurance. They have to keep detailed records of what they earn and spend on the business. ❞

HELP AND ADVICE

Banks can give information and advice on setting up your own business and offer start-up loans, which need to be repaid with interest. Government grants and other financial support may be available. You can get details of these and advice on becoming self-employed from Business Link, a government-funded project for people starting or running a business: www.businesslink.gov.uk telephone: 0845 600 9006.

 For further information on self-employment and setting up your own business, see the Which? Essential Guide *Working for Yourself.*

WORKING IN EUROPE

British citizens can work in any country that is a member of the European Economic Area (EEA). In general, they have the same employment rights as a citizen of that country or state.

Check that you understand:

Equal rights
• The categories covered by the law and exceptions
• Equal job/equal pay regardless of gender
• The different commissions working to promote equal opportunities
• The grounds for sexual harassment complaints

At work
• The important of contracts of employment
• The minimum wage and holiday entitlement
• Information that has to be provided on pay slips

Tax
• What is deducted from your earnings and why
• The difference between being self-employed and employed
• Where to get help if you need it when filling out forms
• The purpose of National Insurance and what happens if you don't pay enough contributions

• How you can get a National Insurance number

Pensions
• Who is entitled to a pension
• What age men and women can get a pension

Health and safety
• Employer and employee obligations
• What to do if you have concerns about health and safety

Trade unions
• What they are and who can join

Losing your job
• Where to go if you need advice on a problem at work
• Possible reasons for dismissal
• The role of Employment Tribunals
• Who can help
• The timescale for complaining
• Entitlement to redundancy pay

Self-employment
• Responsibility for keeping detailed records and paying tax and National Insurance
• The role of Business Link

Childcare and children at work

This section explains your rights as a parent or an expectant mother at work. It also summarises what legal requirements affect children who work and how these are designed to protect them.

In this section there is information about:
• Childcare and children at work

NEW MOTHERS AND FATHERS

Women who are expecting a baby have a legal right to time off work for antenatal care. They are also entitled to at least 26 weeks' maternity leave. These rights apply to full-time and part-time workers and it makes no difference how long the woman has worked for her employer. It is, however, important to follow the correct procedures and to give the employer enough notice about taking maternity leave. Some women may also be entitled to maternity pay but this depends on how long they have been working for their employer.

Fathers who have worked for their employer for at least 26 weeks are entitled to paternity leave, which provides up to two weeks' time off from work, with pay, when the child is born. It is important to tell your employer well in advance.

You can get advice and more information on maternity and paternity matters from the personnel officer at work, your trade union representative, your local Citizens Advice Bureau, the Citizens Advice Bureau website www.adviceguide.org.uk or the government website www.direct.gov.uk

> **!** Most employed women now have the right to take 52 weeks maternity leave. When this official Home Office text, *Life in the United Kingdom: A Journey to Citizenship*, was published maternity leave was still 26 weeks. For the purposes of the Life in the UK Test, however, you need to know the information as outlined in the official text.

Study tip: Avoid caffeine

If you drink lots of coffee or other drinks containing caffeine, it can make you feel more nervous. In addition, coffee is a diuretic. This means that you may want to use the toilet more often, which might make you feel uncomfortable during your test.

CHILDCARE

It is Government policy to help people with childcare responsibilities to take up work. Some employers can help with this. The ChildcareLink website www.childcarelink.gov.uk gives information about different types of childcare and registered childminders in your area, or telephone 08000 96 02 96.

HOURS AND TIME FOR CHILDREN AT WORK

In the UK there are strict laws to protect children from exploitation and to make sure that work does not get in the way of their education. The earliest legal age for children to do paid work is 13, although not all local authorities allow this. There are exceptions for some types of performance work (including modelling) when younger children may be allowed to work. Any child under school leaving age (16) seeking to do paid work must apply for licence from the local authority. Children taking part in some kinds of performances may have to obtain a medical certificate before working.

By law, children under 16 can only do light work. There are particular jobs that children are not allowed to do. These include delivering milk, selling alcohol, cigarettes or medicines, working in a kitchen or behind the counter of a chip shop, working with dangerous machinery or chemicals, or doing any other kind of work that may be harmful to their health or education.

The school leaving age has been changed since this official Home Office text was published. For further details see page 94.

The law sets out clear limits for the working hours and times for 13-16 year old children. Every child must have at least two consecutive weeks a year during the school holidays when they do not work. They cannot work:

- For more than 4 hours without a one-hour rest break
- For more than 2 hours on any school day or a Sunday
- More than five hours (13-14 year olds) or eight hours (15-16 year olds) on Saturdays (or weekdays during school holidays)
- Before 7.00am or after 7.00pm
- Before the close of school hours (except in areas where local bylaws allow children to work one hour before school)
- For more than 12 hours in any school week
- For more than 25 hours a week (13-14 year olds) or 35 hours a week (15-16 year olds) during school holidays.

There is no national minimum wage for those under 16.

" The law sets out clear limits for the working hours and times for 13-16 year old children. An employer may be prosecuted for illegally employing a child. "

The local authority may withdraw a child's licence to work, for example where a child works longer hours than the law allows. The child would then be unable to continue to work. An employer may be prosecuted for illegally employing a child. A parent or carer who makes a false declaration in a child's licence application can also be prosecuted. They may also be prosecuted if they do not ensure their child receives a proper education. You can find more information on the TUC website, www.worksmart.org.uk

 Contact your own local authority for any specific local rules governing the employment of children. To find your local authority, enter your postcode into the search tool at http://local.direct.gov.uk/mycouncil/

Check that you understand

Maternity and paternity rights
- Entitlement to maternity leave and pay for both part time and full-time workers
- Paternity leave entitlement
- The importance of following the right procedures and providing sufficient notice

Children at work
- Minimum age for starting work
- Jobs that children under 16 are not allowed to do
- The maximum hours allowed
- Licence and medical certificate requirements
- The local authority's role in licensing and protecting children in employment
- Parents' responsibilities to ensure that children work within the law and get proper education

Employment

Employment

Practice questions

For the answers to these questions, see page 190.

1 Which of the following statements is correct?
A Employers do NOT have to check that anyone they employ is legally entitled to work in the UK
B Employers have to check that anyone they employ is legally entitled to work in the UK

2 How can you compare qualifications from another country with those in the UK?
A By contacting the National Academic Recognition Information Centre
B By visiting your local library
C By asking your neighbour
D By writing to potential employers

3 True or False? If a job involves working with children the employer will ask for a criminal record check.
A True
B False

4 True or False? In Northern Ireland, the law bans discrimination on grounds of political opinion.
A True
B False

5 Where can you get information on training? (Select two options)
A www.worktrain.gov.uk
B www.learndirect.co.uk
C www.training4work.gov.uk
D www.directlearning.co.uk

6 What details about a job do employers NOT normally provide at the interview?
A Which tax office they use
B Pay
C Holidays
D Working conditions

7 How should you register yourself for tax and National Insurance when you become self-employed?
A Ring your accountant
B Have a lawyer draw up a contract
C Make a note on your next tax return form
D Ring the HM Revenue and Customs telephone helpline

8 True or False? In the eyes of the law, men and women who do the same job should receive equal pay.
A True
B False

9 Which of the following statements is correct?

A Most of the laws protecting people at work apply equally to people doing part-time or full-time jobs

B Most of the laws protecting people at work apply only to people in full-time work

10 For what reasons might you be made redundant? (Select two options)

A Your company no longer needs someone to do your job

B Your company can no longer afford to employ you

C You have been accused of serious misconduct at work

D Your company has found someone better to do your job

11 True or False? Employees have their National Insurance contributions deducted from their pay by their employer.

A True

B False

12 What organisation can give you information on your rights at work?

A The Jobcentre

B The Central Office of Information

C The Passport Office

D The National Advisory, Conciliation and Arbitration Service

13 How many weeks of paid holiday each year are employees over 16 normally entitled to every year?

A Two weeks

B Three weeks

C Four weeks

D Five weeks

14 True or False? All employees are entitled to a written contract of employment.

A True

B False

15 What information must an employer show on pay slips? (Select two options)

A The number of days holiday entitlement that you have remaining

B Tax that has been deducted from your pay

C The date that your contract started

D National Insurance contributions that have been deducted from your pay

16 True or False? If you are made redundant you may be entitled to redundancy pay.

A True

B False

17 Which Government department is responsible for collecting taxes?

A HM Revenue and Customs

B The Department for Work and Pensions

C The Home Office

D The Benefits Agency

18 Which of the following statements is correct?

A Self-employed people need to pay their own tax

B Self-employed people have tax automatically taken from their earnings

19 True or False? Your employer can dismiss you for being a union member.

A True

B False

20 Where can you apply for a National Insurance number? (Select two options)

A Your local library

B Your local Social Security office

C Your local council or town hall

D Any Jobcentre Plus branch

21 True or False? Employers have a legal duty to make sure the workplace is safe.

A True

B False

22 What is the name of the Government-funded project for people starting or running a business?

A Business Connection

B Business Assist

C Business Start-up

D Business Link

23 True or False? British citizens can work in any country that is a member of the European Economic Area (EEA).

A True

B False

24 Which of the following statements is correct?

A Only women that have full-time employment are entitled to maternity leave

B Maternity leave rights apply to both full-time and part-time workers

25 True or False? Most people who become unemployed can claim Jobseeker's Allowance.

A True

B False

26 Which of the following statements is correct?

A Men are always entitled to paternity leave no matter how long they have worked for their employer

B Men must have worked for their employer at least 26 weeks before they are entitled to paternity leave

27 What is the maximum number of hours that a child can work on a school day or Sunday?

A 2 hours

B 4 hours

C 6 hours

D 8 hours

28 Which of the following statements is correct?

A It is illegal to employ children under the age of 13

B Children under the age of 13 are allowed to do some types of performance work (including modelling)

29 What paperwork do children aged 13 to 16 need before they can work? (Select two options)

A A licence from the local authority

B A National Insurance number

C A medical certificate

D Proof of identity

30 Which of the following statements is correct?

A Children are allowed to work for the full duration of their school holidays

B Children must have two consecutive weeks a year during their holidays when they do not work

Knowing the law

UK law is divided into civil and criminal law. It applies equally to everyone, regardless of their background or any crime they are alleged to have committed. This chapter outlines the work of the police and the role of the different courts in the UK. It also looks at the basic legal rights enjoyed by married couples, children and consumers.

The rights and duties of a citizen

As a UK citizen, you enjoy a range of rights enshrined in law. With those rights come responsibilities. These include adhering to the country's laws, reporting a crime and assisting the police in their enquiries.

In this section there is information about:
- The police
- Crime and the law
- Criminal courts

THE LAW

Every person in the UK has the right to equal treatment under the law. The law applies in the same way to everyone – regardless of who they are or where they are from.

The law can be divided into criminal and civil law. Criminal law relates to crimes, which are usually investigated by the police or some other authority and are punished by the courts. Civil law is used to settle disputes between individuals or groups.

In the UK it is a criminal offence to carry a weapon such as a gun or knife or anything that is made or adapted to cause injury to someone, even if it is for self-defence.

❝ In an emergency, or if you are the victim of a crime or you see a crime taking place, dial 999 or 112. Ask for police, fire, ambulance or the coastguard. ❞

REPORTING A CRIME

In an emergency, or if you are the victim of a crime or you see a crime taking place, dial 999 or 112. The operator will ask you which service you need – police, fire, ambulance or, by the coast, the coastguard. Then you need to explain why the police are needed and where they need to go.

If the situation is NOT an emergency, you can either go to your local police station or telephone them. You can find the telephone number under 'Police' in the phone book. Some 'minor' crimes can be reported online. See www.online.police.uk for details.

RACIALLY AND RELIGIOUSLY MOTIVATED CRIME

In the UK it is a criminal offence to use abusive or insulting words in public because of someone's religion or ethnic origin. Anyone who causes harassment, alarm or distress to other people because of their religion or ethnic origin can be prosecuted and given strong penalties by the courts. If you are the victim of religious or racially motivated crime, it is important to report this to the police and they have a duty to take action. You can ask for an interview at the police station, at your home or somewhere else.

You can get further information and advice from the Race Equality Council or from your local Citizens Advice Bureau.

POLICE DUTIES

The job of the police in the UK is to:

- Protect life and property
- Prevent disturbances (known as keeping the peace)
- Prevent and detect crime.

The police force is a public service and should help and protect everyone. You should not be afraid of reporting a crime or asking the police for help. Police officers must obey the law and they must not misuse their authority, make a false statement, be rude, abusive or commit racial discrimination. The very small numbers of police officers who are corrupt or misuse their authority are severely punished.

The Race Equality Council was replaced by the Equality and Human Rights Commission in October 2007. See page 116 for further details.

COMPLAINTS

Anyone can make an official complaint against the police. To make a complaint, you can go to a police station or write to either the Chief Constable for that police force or the Independent Police Complaints Commission (in Northern Ireland, the Police Ombudsman). If it is a serious matter, it is a good idea to speak to a solicitor or to the Citizens Advice Bureau first.

IF THE POLICE EVER STOP YOU

All good citizens are expected to help the police prevent and detect crimes whenever they can. The police can stop any member of the public on foot in connection with a crime that has been committed or is about to take place. They can stop people in a vehicle at any time.

If you are stopped by the police you should give the officer your name and address. You do not need to answer any more questions, although usually people do. You can ask for the name of the officer who stopped and questioned you, the police station where he or she is based and the reason why you have been stopped.

The police can ask you to go to a police station to answer more questions and you can choose whether to go. If you go to a police station voluntarily, you are entitled to leave when you want to. If you are obstructive, rude or decide to mislead the police, you risk being arrested.

❝ All good citizens are expected to help the police prevent and detect crimes. The police can stop anyone in connection with a crime that has been committed or is about to take place. ❞

SEARCH

The police can stop and search anyone they think might be involved in a crime. This includes offences such as theft, burglary or possession of illegal drugs or things to be used for committing criminal damage. They can also search the vehicle of the person they stop.

Police officers do not have the power to enter and search any building they choose, but they can enter a building if they have a warrant (that is special permission from a magistrate, in Scotland a Sheriff), or to arrest someone, to save a life or to prevent serious disturbance or damage. You can ask for the name of the officer who has stopped you, the police station where he or she is based and the reason for their search.

ARREST

If you are arrested and taken to a police station, a police officer will tell you the reason for your arrest.

If you have difficulty in understanding English, the police should provide an interpreter unless they think a delay in finding an interpreter might result in serious harm to a person or property.

The police should normally only interview a young person under the age of 17 if their parent or an 'appropriate adult' is present. This could be a social worker, an adult friend or a teacher.

INFORMATION AND ADVICE

If you are arrested or detained at a police station, you are given written details of three important legal rights:

1 The right to see a solicitor
2 The right to send a message to a friend or a member of your family, telling them where you are
3 The right to look at the codes of practice-guidelines that the police should follow when searching for and collecting evidence.

This written note also includes the official police caution given to all suspects:

You do not have to say anything.
But it may harm your defence if you do not mention,
when questioned, something which you later rely on in court.
Anything you do say may be given in evidence.

This caution means that the police cannot force a person to answer questions. But if a suspect does not answer questions at the police station, or in court, this can be used as evidence against him or her. The caution also states that anything a person does say to a police officer can also be used as evidence in court.

THE DUTY SOLICITOR

Anyone who has been arrested or goes to a police station voluntarily is entitled to legal advice in private. This can be with a solicitor of their choice or the duty solicitor. Duty solicitors work for local firms that specialise in criminal law and offer a free consultation. Usually the advice is given in person but sometimes it may be given over the telephone.

If you have been arrested, or are being questioned about a serious offence, or you feel unsure about your legal position, you have the right not to answer questions (except to give your name and address) until you have spoken to a solicitor.

There are some differences between the court system in England and Wales and the system in Scotland and Northern Ireland.

&&Anyone who has been arrested or goes to a police station voluntarily is entitled to legal advice in private. This can be with a solicitor of their choice or the duty solicitor. ""

MAGISTRATES' AND DISTRICT COURTS

In England, Wales and Northern Ireland most minor criminal cases are dealt with in a magistrates' court. In Scotland, minor criminal offences go to a district court.

Criminal courts

Here is an overview of the courts that deal with both minor and more serious crimes in England, Wales, Northern Ireland and Scotland. It also outlines the rules and practices that are exclusive to courts concerning children and young people.

In this section there is information about:
• Criminal courts

Magistrates, also known as Justices of the Peace, hear less serious cases in magistrates' and district courts. They are members of the local community. In England and Wales they usually work unpaid and have no legal qualifications, although they do receive training. In Northern Ireland, cases are only heard by paid magistrates.

CROWN COURTS AND SHERIFF COURTS
In England, Wales and Northern Ireland, serious offences are tried in front of a judge and a jury in a Crown court. In Scotland, serious cases are heard in a sheriff court with either a sheriff or a sheriff with a jury. A jury is made up of members of the public chosen at random from the local electoral register (see Chapter 4). In England, Wales and Northern Ireland a jury has 12 members, and in Scotland a jury has 15 members. Everyone who is summoned to do jury service must do it unless they are not eligible, for example if they work in law enforcement, or they provide a good reason to be excused, such as ill health. The jury decides on the verdict, that is whether the defendant is innocent or guilty, and if the verdict is guilty the judge decides on the penalty.

YOUTH COURT
If an accused person is 17 years old or younger, their case is normally heard in a youth court in front of up to three specially trained magistrates or a district judge. The most serious cases will go to a Crown court. The parents of the young person are expected to attend the hearing. Members of the public are not allowed in youth courts and neither the name nor the photograph of the young person can be published in newspapers or used by the media. In Scotland there is a unique system called the Children's Hearings System, and Northern Ireland now has a system based on 'youth conferencing'.

Civil courts

Civil courts, including county courts and sheriff courts, deal with minor disputes including small claims procedures, breaches of contract and divorce. This section outlines their role and provides information on how to contact the court for further details.

In this section there is information about:
- Civil courts

COUNTY COURTS

Most towns and cities have a county court to deal with a wide range of civil disputes. These include people trying to get back money that is owed to them, cases involving personal injury, family matters, breaches of contract and divorce. In Scotland, all of these matters are dealt with in the sheriff court.

THE SMALL CLAIMS PROCEDURE

The small claims procedure is an informal way of helping people to settle minor disputes without spending a lot of time and money using a solicitor. This procedure is usually used for claims of less than £5,000. The hearing is held in an ordinary room with a judge and people from both sides of the dispute sitting around a table. You can get details about the small claims procedure from your local county court (in Scotland local sheriff court), which is listed under Courts in the phone book.

66 The small claims procedure is an informal way of helping people to settle minor disputes without spending a lot of time and money using a solicitor. This procedure is usually used for claims of less than £5,000. 99

Legal aid and advice

Depending on the dispute or crime, you may seek legal advice from a solicitor in a variety of ways. This includes contacting a solicitor directly though their practice, or by getting in touch with a law centre or Citizens Advice Bureau.

SOLICITORS

Solicitors are trained lawyers who give advice on legal matters, take action for their clients and represent their clients in court. There are solicitors' offices throughout the UK. It is important to find out which aspects of law a solicitor specialises in and to check that they have the right experience to help you with your case. Many advertise in local papers and the *Yellow Pages*, and the Citizens Advice Bureau can give you names of local solicitors and which areas of law they specialise in. You can also get this information from the Law Society (telephone: 020 7242 1222, www.solicitors-online.com) and the Community Legal Service (telephone 0845 345 4345, www.clsdirect.org.uk).

" There is a Citizens Advice Bureau in most towns and cities. They give free and confidential advice on many different types of legal problems. **"**

COSTS

Solicitors' charges are usually based on how much time they spend on a case. It is very important to find out at the start how much a case is likely to cost and whether you are eligible for legal aid.

FINANCIAL HELP OR LEGAL AID

Anyone who is questioned or charged in connection with a crime is entitled to free advice from a duty solicitor (see above) and free representation by a solicitor for their first appearance in court. It may also be possible to get help with costs for any further appearances in court, although this depends on the type of case and the income and savings of the client. A solicitor can give information and advice on this.

Solicitors can also give information on schemes to cover the cost of a solicitor's help, but not all types of case are covered by these schemes and the help available also depends on the income and savings of the client. Sometimes the costs are paid by the client on a 'no win, no fee' basis. In no win, no fee cases, the solicitor only charges the client if they win the case. It is important to check all the possible costs before agreeing to a solicitor taking a case as no win, no fee, as there are often hidden costs such as paying the costs of the other side.

LAW CENTRES

Most large cities have one or more Law Centres staffed by qualified lawyers. They can give legal advice and possibly take on a case. To find the address of your nearest centre, you can telephone the Law Centres Federation on 020 7387 8570 or visit: www.lawcentres.org.uk

OTHER ADVICE AND INFORMATION

There is a Citizens Advice Bureau in most towns and cities. They give free and confidential advice on many different types of legal problems. Their website also gives a wide range of information in English, Welsh, Bengali, Chinese, Gujarati, Punjabi and Urdu: www.adviceguide.org.uk

JUST ASK!

www.clsdirect.org.uk is the website of the Community Legal Service and it gives information on a wide range of legal questions in seven languages. It can also give you details of local solicitors and places to go for advice in your area.

❝ It is important to check all the possible costs before agreeing to a solicitor taking a case as no win, no fee, as there are often hidden costs such as paying the costs of the other side. ❞

FOR TEENAGERS

The Young Citizen's Passport is a practical guide to everyday law written especially for the needs of young people aged 14 to 19. It is produced by the Citizenship Foundation and there are three different editions:

England and Wales, Scotland and Northern Ireland. You can order a copy through a local bookshop or telephone the publishers, Hodder Murray, on 020 7837 6372.

VICTIMS OF CRIME

Anyone who is the victim of a violent crime can apply to the Criminal Injuries Compensation Authority for compensation for their injuries. The crime has to be reported to the police as quickly as possible and the application for compensation must be made within two years of the crime. You can find more information on the Criminal Injuries Compensation Authority website: www.cica.gov.uk

Victims of crime can also get free help and guidance from Victim Support. You can find their telephone number in the local phone book, ring their national helpline on 0845 30 30 900 or go to their website: www.victimsupport.com

Check that you understand
- How the police force is organised and the responsibilities of the police
- How to report a crime
- Your rights if you are stopped and searched or arrested
- How to make a complaint about the police and get support if you are the victim of a crime
- That it is illegal for you to carry a weapon
- The different types of criminal and civil courts
- How to get legal advice and legal aid

Human rights

Everyone in the UK has their personal rights protected by the Human Rights Act, 1988. This section defines what these rights include, as well as the responsibilities of citizens to avoid compromising the rights of others, in particular laws regarding marriage and same-sex partnerships.

In this section there is information about:
- Human rights
- Marriage and divorce

THE HUMAN RIGHTS ACT

All UK courts must follow the principles of the European Convention on Human Rights. These rights are set out in British law in the Human Rights Act 1998 and apply to everyone in the UK. Public bodies such as the police, schools and hospitals have to work in a way that follows the Human Rights Act.

There is more general information on the Human Rights Act on the Department of Constitutional Affairs website: www.dca.gov.uk/peoples-rights/human-rights/index.htm

In Northern Ireland there is a Human Rights Commission, which is considering whether Northern Ireland needs its own additional human rights law. It also works with its counterpart in the Republic of Ireland with the aim of achieving common standards in both parts of the island.

EQUAL OPPORTUNITIES

For more than 30 years the law in the UK has been developed to try and make sure that people are not treated unfairly in all areas of life and work because of their sex, race, disability, sexuality or religion. In 2006 unfair age discrimination at work also became unlawful.

If you face problems with discrimination, you can get more information from the Citizens Advice Bureau or from one of the following organisations:

The Commission for Racial Equality – www.cre.gov.uk
The Equal Opportunities Commission – www.eoc.org.uk

The Human Rights Act lists 16 basic rights (the 'Convention Rights'):

- **The right to life** – Everyone has the right for their life to be protected by the law. The state can only take someone's life in very limited circumstances, such as when a police officer acts justifiably in self-defence.
- **Prohibition of torture** – No one should be tortured or punished or treated in an inhuman or degrading way.
- **Prohibition of slavery and forced labour** – No one should be held in slavery or forced to work.
- **The right to liberty and security** – Everyone has the right not to be detained or have their liberty taken away, unless it is within the law and the correct legal procedures are followed.
- **The right to a fair trial** – Everyone has the right to a fair trial and a public hearing within a reasonable period of time. Everyone charged with a criminal offence is presumed innocent until proved guilty.
- **No punishment without law** – No one should be found guilty of an offence that was not a crime at the time it was committed.
- **Right to respect a person's private and family life** – Everyone has the right for their private and family life, their home and their correspondence to be respected. There should not be any interference with this unless there are very good reasons, such as state security, public safety or the prevention of a crime.
- **Freedom of thought, conscience and religion** – Everyone is free to hold whatever views and beliefs they wish. Again, this right is only limited for reasons such as public safety, the protection of public order and the protection of the freedom and rights of others.
- **Freedom of expression** – Everyone has the freedom to express their views. This may, however, be limited for reasons of public safety or to protect the rights of others.
- **Freedom of assembly and association** – Everyone has the right to get together with other people in a peaceful way. This again may be limited for reasons of public safety or to protect the rights of others.
- **Right to marry** – Men and women have the right to marry and start a family, but national law may put restrictions on when this may take place and with whom.
- **Prohibition of discrimination** – Everyone is entitled to the rights and freedoms set out in the European Convention on Human Rights. This is regardless of their race, sex, language, religion, political opinion, national or social origin or for any other reason.
- **Protection of property** – No one should be deprived of their possessions except in the public interest, such as when the state raises taxes or confiscates goods that are unlawful or dangerous.
- **The right to education** – No one should be denied the right to education.
- **The right to free elections** – Elections for government must be free, fair and take place at reasonable intervals with a secret ballot.
- **Prohibition of the death penalty** – No one can be condemned to death or executed.

The Disability Rights Commission – www.drc.org.uk
(These three organisations will be brought together in the
Commission for Equality and Human Rights from October 2007).
The Equality Commission for Northern Ireland – www.equalityni.org

For further information on discrimination at work, see chapter 6.

MILITARY SERVICE
In the UK there has been no compulsory military service since 1960.

MARRIAGE
In order to marry, each partner must be 16 years old or older, and
unmarried. Anyone who is 16 or 17 and wants to get married needs
written permission from their parents. Close blood relatives are not
allowed to marry each other although cousins are allowed to marry.
No one can be forced to get married regardless of how strong the
wishes of their family may be. Couples who have agreed to marry
usually announce their engagement. In the past an engagement was
seen as a legal contract but these days it is not.

A marriage ceremony can take place in a registry office, a registered
place of worship or in premises that have been approved by the local
authority. You can get a list of these from your local authority.

**❝ In order to marry, each partner must be 16 years
old or older, and unmarried. Anyone who is 16 or 17
and wants to get married needs written permission
from their parents. ❞**

In order for a marriage ceremony to take place, couples need to get
certificates from the registrar of marriages in the district(s) where they
live. In order to get a certificate, the partners need to show their birth
certificates or, if these are not available, their personal identity

For further information on registering a marriage in England and Wales see the
General Register Office, www.gro.gov.uk. For the General Register Office for Scotland
see www.gro-scotland.gov.uk. For the General Register Office (Northern Ireland)
see www.groni.gov.uk

documents. If either of the partners has been married before, they need to show proof that this marriage has ended. Certificates can be collected between 21 days and 3 months before the date of the wedding.

The procedure for marriages in the Church of England is slightly different. The traditional method used by most couples is the publication of banns, which takes the same time as the civil method of getting married by certificate. The banns are published by being read aloud during the service on each of the three Sundays before the ceremony. You do not have to be a member of the church to be married there but it is usual for the couple to attend the church on at least one of the three occasions when the banns are read. You can get more details from either a religious minister who is authorised to conduct marriages or the local registrar of marriages - see Registration of births, marriages and deaths in the phone book.

In the UK, many women take their husband's surname when they get married. But there is no legal duty to do this and some women prefer to keep their own surname.

LIVING TOGETHER

These days, many couples in the UK live together without getting married or live together before they get married. Couples who live together without being married do not have the same legal rights as couples who are married and may face some problems if their relationship breaks up. For example, if only one partner's name is on a tenancy agreement or title deeds to a property, the other partner may have difficulty staying in a property or claiming a share in its value.

❝ Couples who live together without being married do not have the same legal rights as couples who are married and may face some problems if their relationship breaks up. ❞

If a married person dies without making a will, their husband or wife is entitled to all or most of their possessions. But if a couple are not married and there is no will, it can be very difficult for the surviving partner to claim any of their partner's possessions.

If an unmarried couple have a child, both parents have a duty to support that child until he or she is 18 years old.

SAME-SEX PARTNERSHIPS

Couples of the same sex can now legally register their relationship and mark this with a civil ceremony known as a civil partnership. When they do this they have similar legal rights to those of married couples.

DIVORCE

Divorce cannot take place during the first year of marriage. In order for a man or a woman to apply for a divorce they must prove to a court that their marriage has 'irretrievably broken down'. In order to do this, he or she must prove one of the following things has happened:

- Their partner has committed adultery
- Their partner has behaved unreasonably. This can cover many things such as domestic violence, assault, or refusing to have children
- They have lived apart for two years and both want a divorce
- They have lived apart for five years and only one partner wants a divorce
- One partner has deserted the other for at least two years before the application for divorce.

❝ If you are facing divorce, or if your partner has left you, it is very important to get advice about your legal position from a solicitor, particularly if you have young children or if there is disagreement over money or property. ❞

HELP AND ADVICE

The breakdown of a marriage can be a very difficult time for everyone involved. Family doctors can sometimes help by arranging an appointment with a family therapist. There is also a voluntary and independent

 For further information on the process of separation or divorce, see the Which? Essential Guide, *Divorce and Splitting Up*.

organisation called Relate, which operates in England and Wales. You can find their contact details in the phone book under Relate or at www.relate.org.uk

If you are facing divorce, or if your partner has left you, it is very important to get advice about your legal position from a solicitor, particularly if you have young children or if there is disagreement over money or property.

DOMESTIC VIOLENCE

In the UK, brutality and violence in the home is a serious crime. Anyone who is violent towards their partner - whether they are a man or a woman, married or living together - can be prosecuted. Any man who forces a woman to have sex, including a woman's husband, can be charged with rape.

It is important for any woman in this situation to get help as soon as possible. A solicitor or the Citizens Advice Bureau can explain the available options. In some areas there are safe places for women to go and stay in called refuges or shelters. There are emergency telephone numbers in the Helpline section at the front of the *Yellow Pages* including, for women, the number of the nearest Women's Centre. The police can also help women find a safe place to stay.

Children

Both parents have responsibilities when it coms to caring for and supporting their children. This section outlines issues such as child protection, medical advice for young people and the laws governing when a child may be left on his or her own.

In this section there is information about:
- Children and young people

PARENTS' RESPONSIBILITIES

The law says that parents of a child who are married to one another have equal responsibility for their child. This continues even if the parents separate or divorce. But when a child's parents are not married, only the mother has parental responsibility unless:

- The father jointly registers the child's birth with the mother
- The father subsequently marries the mother
- The father obtains the mother's agreement for equal parental responsibility
- The father acquires parental responsibility by applying to court.

Parental responsibility continues until a child is 18 years old.

❝ The law says that parents of a child who are married to one another have equal responsibility for their child. This continues even if the parents separate or divorce. ❞

SUPPORT

Both parents, whether they are married to each other or not, have a legal responsibility to maintain their children financially. A father who does not have parental responsibility in law still has a duty to support his children financially.

CONTROL

Parents are responsible for the care and control of their children until they are 18. By law, they can use reasonable force to discipline them, but if this punishment is too severe, they can be prosecuted for assault or the child may be taken into the care of the local authority.

Many voluntary organisations and local authorities offer parenting courses, support and advice on being a parent. Parentline Plus is a national charity that works for, and with, parents. They offer a free 24-hour, 7 days a week telephone helpline service for parents – telephone: 0808 800 202, or www.parentlineplus.org.uk You can also get information on parenting on the BBC website: www.bbc.co.uk/parenting

❝ If a young person under the age of 16 asks for contraceptive advice and treatment, the doctor will encourage them to discuss this with a parent or carer. ❞

CHILD PROTECTION

Every local authority has a legal duty to protect all children in its area from danger, and must place the safety and interest of the child above all else. If it believes that a child is suffering significant harm at home, it must take action to try and stop this happening. Where possible, local authorities try to work with parents, but they have the power to take a child from its home and into care. This is only done in an emergency or when all other possibilities have failed.

ChildLine is a free and confidential helpline for children and young people in the UK to talk about any problem with a counsellor-telephone 0800 1111, or: www.childline.org.uk. In the UK, there are laws about employment and children (see Chapter 6).

MEDICAL ADVICE AND TREATMENT FOR CHILDREN AND YOUNG PEOPLE

From the age of 16, young people do not need their parents' permission for medical consultation or treatment as long as the doctor or nurse believes that the young person fully understands what is involved.

If a young person under the age of 16 asks for contraceptive advice and treatment, the doctor will encourage them to discuss this with a parent or carer. But most doctors will prescribe contraception for a young person if they believe they are able to understand what is involved.

LEAVING A CHILD ON THEIR OWN

As a general rule, it is against the law for children to be left alone in the home unless they are in the care of a responsible person aged 16 or over.

Childminders and nurseries must be registered and inspected by the Office for Standards in Education (Ofsted). You can get details of registered childminders in your area from your local authority, Children's Information Service (CIS). ChildcareLink on 08000 96 02 96 or www.childcarelink.gov.uk can give you the telephone number of your local CIS. You can also contact the National Childminding Association (NCMA) on 0800 169 4486 or www.ncma.org.uk

Check that you understand
- What the Human Rights Act is
- What equal opportunities means and how to get more information about it
- The laws about marriage, divorce and domestic violence
- The laws about parental responsibility for children
- How to get support about parenting
- Children's rights and support for children and young people

Consumer protection

Everyone who buys certain types of goods and services in the UK enjoys a number of legally enforceable guarantees and protections. This section indicates which areas are covered by law and which are not, and the steps you can take if you receive faulty goods.

In this section there is information about:
- Consumer protection

By law, when you buy something from a shop, it should do everything you can reasonably expect and all that the seller and manufacturer claim. The Sale of Goods Act 1979 states that the goods you buy from a shop or trader must:

- Be of satisfactory quality, and
- Match the description, and
- Be fit for all their intended purposes.

SATISFACTORY QUALITY

'Being of satisfactory quality' means the goods must be free from faults, scratches or damage – unless the sales assistant told you about the fault or you had a chance to look carefully at the item before you bought it and had the opportunity to find the fault.

“By law, when you buy something from a shop, it should do everything you can reasonably expect and all that the seller and manufacturer claim.”

This rule applies to any goods you buy from a shop or trader – new or second-hand. But it does not apply to goods bought privately from an individual, for example through a newspaper or shop window advertisement. In these cases, the buyer is expected to take responsibility for the quality of the goods they buy.

MATCH THE DESCRIPTION

'Matching the description' means that the goods you buy must be the same as the description on the packaging or advertisement at the time of sale. This rule applies to all goods sold, including second-hand goods sold privately.

FIT FOR ALL THEIR INTENDED PURPOSES

'Being fit for all their intended purposes' means that the goods must do what the seller, packaging or advertiser claims.

❝ Prices are usually clearly marked on most new goods and these are the prices that customers expect to pay. In general, people in the UK do not barter or negotiate prices for goods. ❞

TAKING CARE WITH YOUR PURCHASES

Sometimes there are problems with goods bought from shops, by mail order or on the internet and so it is a good idea to take the following steps:

- Be cautious of advertisements that make exaggerated claims, and of people who try to sell you things at your door
- Keep receipts as proof of purchase, particularly if the goods were expensive
- If there is a problem with something you bought, stop using it straight away and tell the shop or trader about the problem
- If you have to make a complaint to a shop or company, keep a record of telephone calls and make a copy of any letters or emails that you send.

Prices are usually clearly marked on most new goods and these are the prices that customers expect to pay. In general, people in the UK do not barter or negotiate prices for goods. But some bargaining may take place when buying houses, second-hand goods such as cars, or some household services such as decorating or gardening.

SERVICES

The law covering services – such as hairdressing or shoe repairs – states that services must be done:

- With reasonable care and skill
- Within a reasonable time
- For a reasonable charge.

To avoid problems it is a good idea to agree the price before the work starts.

MAIL ORDER AND INTERNET SHOPPING

There are special regulations to protect people who buy goods from home, by post, phone or on the internet. As well as the rights listed above, you are entitled to cancel your order within 7 working days if you decide that you do not want to buy the item. But this does not apply to all purchases. For example, you cannot change your mind for tickets or accommodation bookings, audio and video recordings that have been opened, newspapers and magazines, and perishable items such as flowers or food. You are also entitled to a full refund if you do not receive the goods by the date agreed or within 30 days, if you did not agree a date.

If you are buying goods on the internet, it is important to make sure that you have the trader's full address. You also need to make sure that the website offers a secure way of paying – this is shown by a small picture of a yellow padlock at the bottom of the screen.

COMPLAINTS

If a fault appears soon after you have bought an item and you are not responsible you are entitled either to your money back or to a replacement. It is the shop's responsibility to deal with the problem.

If an item worked well at first and then developed a fault, you may still be entitled to all or some of your money back, to be offered a replacement or have the item repaired free of charge. The action taken will depend on how long you have had the goods, how serious the fault is and whether it is unreasonable for a fault to develop so soon.

PAYING BY CREDIT CARD

If you have used a credit card to buy something which cost between £100 and £30,000 and there is a problem with it, you can claim the money from the credit card company. This can be useful if the trader does not help to solve the problem or has gone out of business.

Associations supporting consumer rights

- **Trading Standards Central** – Provides local advice for the consumer as well as having an investigative role.
  Website: www.tradingstandards.gov.uk
- **Consumer Direct** – Government-funded online and telephone service offering advice and information on consumer issues.
  Tel: 08454 040506 Website: www.consumerdirect.gov
- **UK European Consumer Centre** – Information and support for consumers shopping across the EU.
  Tel: 08456 040503 Website: www.ukecc.net
- **Citizens Advice Bureau** – Free local advisory service designed to help people with their legal and money problems.
  Website: www.citizensadvice.org.uk
- **Which?** – Campaigning organisation that defends consumer rights and provides independent advice on products and services through its website, magazines and books.
  Tel: 01992 822800 Website: www.which.co.uk

HELP AND ADVICE

You can get advice locally from the Trading Standards Office, listed in the phone book under the local authority, or from the Citizens Advice Bureau.

You can check the prices and performance of many products in *Which?* an independent magazine. You can subscribe to the magazine or read it in the reference department of most public libraries.

There is more information about consumer rights from the BBC website: www.bbc.co.uk. You can also get information from the government's official department which protects consumers – the Office of Fair Trading, www.oft.gov.uk

---

Check that you understand
- Consumer rights for items bought in shops and by mail order, phone or on the internet
- Consumer rights for services
- How to make complaints and get help and advice

Practice tests

The 10 practice tests provided here echo the format of the real Home Office tests by containing 24 questions each. The actual test takes 45 minutes. Give yourself the same time limit for each of these tests. This will help you work within the time limit when it comes to taking the real test. The answers are listed in Chapter 9.

Test 1

For the answers to test 1 see page 191.

1 What is the name of the tax you must have to drive your car on public roads?
A Drivers' tax
B Road tax
C Car driving tax
D MOT tax

2 Why did many Irish people migrate to the British mainland in the mid-1840s?
A To escape a terrible famine
B To live with their relatives
C To escape religious persecution
D To farm the land

3 Who is entitled to apply for council accommodation?
A Everyone
B The homeless
C People with chronic ill health
D People with children

4 At what voltage is electricity supplied in the UK?
A 110 volts
B 115 volts
C 220 volts
D 240 volts

5 Prior to 2009, at what ages did children in England and Scotland take Key Stage national tests (SATs) in English, mathematics and science?
A 4 years old, 8 years old and 10 years old
B 6 years old, 9 years old and 13 years old
C 7 years old, 11 years old and 14 years old
D 8 years old, 12 years old and 16 years old

6 True or False? Some researchers think that one reason why so few first-time voters use their vote is because young people are not interested in the political process.
A True
B False

7 How is census information collected?
A Respondents complete and return a form that is delivered to every household in the country
B Census takers visit every household and ask a number of questions
C There is a website that requests the information
D Householders have to go to their Town Hall to report their details

8 Which of these statements is correct?

A There are many variations in culture and language in the different parts of the United Kingdom

B There are no variations in culture and language in the different parts of the United Kingdom

9 Which of the following countries would NOT be defined as an 'old' Commonwealth country?

A New Zealand

B Canada

C Russia

D Australia

10 Which of the following have been linked to the use of hard drugs (such as crack cocaine and heroin)? (Select two options)

A Mental illness

B Sleeping

C Eating a lot

D Crime

11 Who led the plan to kill the King with a bomb in the Houses of Parliament on 5 November 1605?

A Guy Fawkes

B King James I

C Oliver Cromwell

D Ben Jonson

12 What is a trade union?

A An organisation to help small businesses

B An organisation that aims to improve the pay and working conditions of its members

C Part of the Trading Standards department

D Part of the tax office

13 What type of constitution does the UK have?

A A written constitution

B A legal constitution

C An unwritten constitution

D An amended constitution

14 Who appoints Life Peers?

A The Queen

B The Prime Minister

C The Archbishop of Canterbury

D The Lord Chancellor

15 What does money raised from NI contributions NOT pay for? (Select two options)

A The State Retirement Pension

B The National Health Service

C Education

D The Police

16 Who do you need to contact if you want to register to vote?

A The local council election registration office

B The local Labour Party

C The public library

D The police station

17 What is the name for a loan that you use to buy a property?

A Mortgage

B Bank loan

C Endowment

D Annuity

18 How long does a television licence last?

A 3 months

B 6 months

C 9 months

D 12 months

19 True or False? There are some jobs where discrimination laws do not apply.

A True

B False

20 What can happen if a member state of the EU persistently refuses to obey the European Convention on Human Rights?

A Nothing: it is not a binding document

B Ministers are called to a meeting at the Council of Europe

C The country is suspended from the Council of Europe for a short period of time

D The country is expelled from the Council of Europe

21 What do the initials NHS stand for?

A New Homes Show

B National Housing Service

C National Hockey Stadium

D National Health Service

22 What is NOT normally accepted as proof of identity?

A A provisional or full driving licence

B A rent book

C A benefits book

D A cheque book

23 True or False? It is legal to be drunk in public.

A True

B False

24 When did the UK join the Council of Europe?

A 1949

B 1953

C 1969

D 1973

Test 2

For the answers to test 2 see page 191.

1 True or False? After the Second World War there was a huge task of rebuilding Britain.
A True
B False

2 During the 1980s which regions did the largest immigrant groups come from?
A South America, Canada, North Africa and Hong Kong
B China, Sri Lanka, Singapore and Malaysia
C Russia, Ethiopia, Uganda and South East Asia
D United States, Australia, South Africa, and New Zealand

3 When were women over 30 given the right to vote?
A 1908
B 1918
C 1928
D 1938

4 What are AS levels?
A Advanced Standard qualifications
B Advanced Subsidiary qualifications
C Advanced Service qualifications
D Advanced Schooling qualifications

5 What is meant by a Free Press?
A Radio and television do not cost anything
B What is written in newspapers is free from government control
C Politicians do not get paid for interviews
D Information is given away for nothing

6 According to the 2001 census, what percentage of the people in the United Kingdom are of Indian descent?
A 0.8%
B 1.8%
C 2.8%
D 3.8%

7 In what part of the UK is the Gaelic language spoken?
A Cornwall
B Scotland and Northern Ireland
C Wales
D England

8 How many bank and public holidays does the UK have?
A 2
B 4
C 6
D 8

9 What might you need to complete or provide when applying for a job? (Select two options)

A Your curriculum vitae

B Proof of your age

C Proof of a bank account

D An application form and covering letter

10 When does the Queen make an official speech?

A To summarise the Government's policies for the year ahead at the opening of each new parliamentary session

B In a weekly broadcast to her subjects

C When a new Government is formed

D Each St George's Day

11 By what system are Members of the European Parliament elected?

A Instant runoff

B Proportional representation

C First past the post

D Multiseat representation

12 What is the leader of the political party in power called?

A The First Minister

B The Prime Minister

C The Chancellor of the Exchequer

D The Home Secretary

13 What happened to the general population's size in the last 20 years?

A There has been a general increase in the population

B There has been no change in the population

C There has been a general decrease of the population

D There has been an increase in the number of female births

14 What is the FA Cup?

A Football Cup Final

B Fancy Acrobatics Cup

C Federation Athletics Meeting

D Formula Air Race

15 What are the names of the Houses of Parliament? (Select two options)

A The House of Commons

B The House of Big Ben

C The House of Westminster

D The House of Lords

16 What proportion of people in the UK own their own home?

A Half

B Three-quarters

C Two-thirds

D One-third

17 True or False? If you do not pay your electricity bill and the supply is cut off, you can be reconnected for free.

A True

B False

18 What is the highest denomination bank note in the UK?

A £10

B £20

C £50

D £100

19 What is a health visitor?

A Someone who works in a hospital/health centre and who provides health support

B A specialist child doctor at the surgery

C A qualified nurse who can advise you about your baby

D A midwife

20 Which of these statements is correct?

A State education in the UK is free

B State education in the UK is paid for by parents and a Government subsidy

---

21 Within what time period of starting a new job should all employees be given a written contract of employment?

A 2 weeks

B 2 months

C 1 year

D 2 years

---

22 True or False? As soon as you become self-employed you should register yourself for tax and National Insurance with HM Revenue and Customs.

A True

B False

---

23 Which of these statements is correct?

A The National Insurance number is a unique number for each person

B One National Insurance number is issued per family

---

24 What is the State Pension age for women?

A 55

B 60

C 65

D 70

Test 3

For the answers to test 3 see page 191.

1 **What countries did Jewish people who came to Britain between 1810 and 1910 to escape racist attacks come from?**
A Poland, Latvia and Lithuania
B Poland, Ukraine and Belarus
C Poland, Hungary and Romania
D Poland, Russia and France

2 **When did a woman's earnings, property and money stop automatically becoming her husband's when she got married?**
A 1682
B 1782
C 1882
D 1982

3 **Can judges change an Act of Parliament if it is incompatible with the Human Rights Act?**
A No, but they can ask Parliament to consider doing so
B Yes, but they must first seek the Prime Minister's approval
C Yes, but only if they believe the law is unfair
D Yes, but they must obtain permission from the Lord Chancellor

4 **Why did Britain admit thousands of people of Indian origin in 1972?**
A To set up new businesses
B To escape religious persecution
C They were forced to leave Uganda
D So that they could join up with their families in Britain

5 **What percentage of children live with both birth parents?**
A 35%
B 45%
C 55%
D 65%

6 **What is the minimum age that you can buy tobacco products in the UK?**
A 14
B 16
C 18
D 21

7 **What percentage of the people of the United Kingdom lived in Scotland in 2005?**
A 8%
B 18%
C 28%
D 38%

8 Where do most of the population of Britain live?

A In villages and hamlets

B Close to the sea

C Within easy reach of a motorway

D In towns and cities

9 What is ONE of the dialects spoken in Northern Ireland?

A Belfast Brogue

B Ulster English

C Stormont Slang

D Ulster Scots

10 What flower is worn in memory of those who died in wars?

A The rose

B The carnation

C The poppy

D The tulip

11 What are the British systems of Government? (Select two options)

A A constitutional democracy

B A federal government

C A legal democracy

D A parliamentary democracy

12 When was the Welsh Assembly established?

A 1997

B 1998

C 1999

D 2000

13 Who do you contact to find out which company supplies your property with gas?

A Your local authority

B Energywatch

C Transco

D British Gas

14 Where do local authorities get most of their funding from?

A Lottery grants

B Issuing parking tickets

C Government taxation

D Local council tax

15 True or False? Everyone has the legal right to practise the religion of their choice.

A True

B False

16 Who is the head of the Commonwealth?

A The Foreign Secretary

B The Prime Minister

C The Queen

D The Lord Chancellor

17 True or False? In Scotland, the agreement to buy a property becomes legally binding earlier than it does elsewhere in the UK.

A True

B False

18 What will happen if you do not pay the total amount of your monthly credit card bill?

A You will be charged interest

B You will receive a reminder letter

C You will be unable to use the card until the bill is paid

D You will be required to return the card to the credit card company

19 Which of the two statements is correct?

A Some dentists have two sets of charges, both NHS and private

B All dentists work for the NHS

165

20 How much does education at state schools in the UK cost?

A £100 per month

B £200 per month

C £500 per month

D Nothing, it is free

21 Which type of people are suitable as job referees? (Select two options)

A Personal friends

B Current or previous employer

C Members of your family

D College tutors

22 True or False? Employers who pay their workers below the minimum wage are breaking the law.

A True

B False

23 Who gives free advice about both occupational and personal pensions?

A The Pensions Advisory Service

B The Pension Service Helpline

C Jobcentre Plus

D The Social Security Office

24 Which of the following statements is correct?

A It is illegal for a child to work before 7am or after 7pm

B Children are free to work at any time of the day

Test 4

For the answers to test 4 see page 191.

1 When were immigrants from the West Indies first actively invited to come to the United Kingdom?
A 1928
B 1938
C 1948
D 1958

2 What is one of the main reasons for the global rise in mass migration since 1994?
A Political and economic reasons
B Social and geographic reasons
C Educational and training reasons
D Ancestry and family reasons

3 True or False? Many young people move away from their family home when they become adults.
A True
B False

4 According to the 2001 census, what proportion of London is of ethnic minority descent?
A Nearly a quarter
B Nearly a third
C Nearly a half
D Nearly two-thirds

5 True or False? Cigarette smoking in Britain has increased among adults.
A True
B False

6 What date is Valentine's Day?
A 1 December
B 7 January
C 14 February
D 21 March

7 What percentage of the population in England is estimated to attend religious services?
A Around 5%
B Around 10%
C Around 15%
D Around 20%

8 When looking for employment, what is the purpose of a referee?
A To negotiate pay after a successful interview
B To write a report about a person's suitability for a job
C To search for jobs that match your skills
D To resolve any disputes between you and your employer

9 Where does the European Parliament meet? (Select two options)

A Geneva

B Brussels

C London

D Strasbourg

10 When is Hogmanay?

A 24 December

B 25 December

C 31 December

D 1 January

11 True or False? The Whips are a small group of MPs responsible for discipline and attendance of MPs at voting time in the House of Commons.

A True

B False

12 What are members of the House of Lords known as?

A Peers

B Nobles

C Royalty

D Knights

13 What is a civil servant?

A A member of a political party

B A Member of Parliament

C A manager or administrator who works for the House of Lords

D A manager or administrator who carries out Government policy

14 What does discrimination in the workplace NOT include?

A Weight

B Sex

C Nationality or race

D Colour or ethnic group

15 True or False? Many other languages in addition to English are spoken in the UK.

A True

B False

16 What do quangos do?

A Carry out functions on behalf of the public

B Review asylum cases

C Test the safety of cars

D Collect taxes

17 When you make an offer on a property, what does the solicitor do? (Select two options)

A Carry out a number of legal checks on the property, the seller and the local area

B Arrange a mortgage for you with a bank

C Provide the legal agreements necessary for you to buy the property

D Checks the structural condition of the property

18 True or False? Landlords are allowed to refuse to rent to people because of their sex, race, nationality, ethnic group or disability.

A True

B False

19 How old must you be to be able to buy a lottery ticket?

A 16

B 17

C 18

D 21

20 True or False? Before you can get a driving licence you must pass a test.

A True

B False

21 What was the population of Wales
   in 2005?

A 2.9 million

B 3.9 million

C 4.9 million

D 5.9 million

---

22 True or False? The death rate is
   falling in the UK.

A True

B False

---

23 What are National Insurance
   contributions used for?
   (Select two options)

A To contribute to your state
   retirement pension

B To pay for police and armed services

C To pay for education and community
   services

D To help fund the National Health
   Service

---

24 How should you register yourself
   for tax and National Insurance when
   you become self-employed?

A Ring your accountant

B Have a lawyer draw up a contract

C Make a note on your next tax return
   form

D Ring the HM Revenue and Customs
   telephone helpline

Test 5

For the answers to test 5 see page 191.

1 **What should you NOT do if you are involved in a road accident?**
A Get the names, addresses, registration numbers and insurance details of the other drivers
B Give your details to the other drivers
C Contact your insurance company
D Leave the scene

2 **During the 1950s, what countries did textile and engineering firms from the UK send recruitment agents to in order to find workers? (Select two options)**
A India
B Pakistan
C Singapore
D Nigeria

3 **What is a gap year?**
A A year that has 366 days instead of 365 days
B A year off work in order to study full-time
C A year of higher education without paying fees
D A year out of education that often includes voluntary work and travel overseas

4 **How many refugees from South East Asia have been allowed to settle in the UK since 1979?**
A More than 10,000
B More than 15,000
C More than 25,000
D More than 50,000

5 **When does a by-election take place?**
A When the Prime Minister wants a new MP
B At least every five years
C When an MP resigns or dies in office
D When the Prime Minister loses a vote of confidence

6 **What information was NOT collected as part of the 2001 census?**
A Age
B Place of birth
C Earnings
D Occupation

7 **True or False? At Christmas time, people usually spend the day at home and eat a special meal, which often includes turkey.**
A True
B False

8 Where are jobs NOT usually advertised?

A Local and national newspapers

B The local library

C The local Jobcentre

D In employment agencies

9 True or False? Education for children in Britain is compulsory.

A True

B False

10 What sport is played at the Open?

A Football

B Rugby

C Tennis

D Golf

11 What does the Scottish Parliament NOT legislate on?

A Education

B Planning

C Foreign affairs

D Raising of additional taxes

12 Which people are NOT usually entitled to receive welfare benefits?

A The sick and disabled

B Older people

C The unemployed and those on low incomes

D People who do not have legal rights of residence in the UK

13 Where can you get more information on criminal record checks? (Select two options)

A From the local police station

B From the Home Office Criminal Records Bureau information line

C From the Citizens Advice Bureau

D From Disclosure Scotland

14 What type of property is council tax NOT applied to?

A Greenhouses

B Maisonettes

C Mobile homes

D Houseboats

15 True or False? The UN Security Council recommends action by the UN when there are international crises and threats to peace.

A True

B False

16 Where can you get mortgage advice? (Select two options)

A From a bank

B From your local council

C From a building society

D From an estate agent

17 Where can you get foreign currency? (Select two options)

A Banks

B Police stations

C Some post offices

D The Foreign Office

18 Where can you get advice about contraception and sexual health?

A From the Citizens Advice Bureau

B From the Family Planning Association (FPA)

C From the local council

D From a fitness centre

19 True or False? Discrimination laws also apply when the job involves working for someone in their own home.

A True

B False

171

20 What is a CV?

A Correct Version

B Classic Verdict

C Church Verger

D Curriculum Vitae

21 True or False? Students can enrol on an AGCE or Scottish Higher/Advanced Higher course without passing any GCSEs or SQA Standard Grades.

A True

B False

22 What TWO bodies make up the legislative body of the EU? (Select two options)

A The Council of the European Union

B The European Parliament

C The European Economic Community

D The European Commission

23 For what TWO reasons can a parent or carer be prosecuted? (Select two options)

A For allowing their child to work

B For making a false declaration on their child's licence to work

C For not insisting their child eats school meals

D For not ensuring their child receives a proper education

24 Which of the following statements is true?

A There is a United Kingdom football team

B Each of the four countries of the UK have their own football team

Test 6

For the answers to test 6 see page 192.

1 Which of the following statements is correct?
A Children under 12 years old do not need to wear a seat belt
B Children under 12 years old should wear a seat belt but may also need a special booster seat

2 When did the Government pass new laws to restrict immigration to Britain?
A 1840s and 1850s
B 1920s and 1930s
C 1960s and 1970s
D 1990s and 2000s

3 What activity do children in the UK NOT do as much as they did in the past?
A Watch television
B Watch videos
C Play computer games
D Play outside

4 What is 11 November officially known as?
A Freedom Day
B Memory Day
C Remembrance Day
D Peace Day

5 True or False? It is widely accepted that drug misuse carries a huge social and financial cost to the country.
A True
B False

6 Which of these statements is correct?
A The different regions in Britain are identifiable by differences in accent and dialect
B The different regions in Britain cannot be identified by differences in accent and dialect

7 True or False? At Christmas time, people often give each other gifts and send each other cards.
A True
B False

8 If you need to stay overnight in a hospital, what items will you need to take with you? (Select two options)
A Food
B Bedding
C A towel and things for washing
D Night clothes

173

9 What sport is played at the Wimbledon tournament?

A Golf

B Cricket

C Tennis

D Football

10 True or False? The monarch makes the final decision on Government policies.

A True

B False

11 By what system are members of the House of Commons elected?

A Instant runoff

B Proportional representation

C First past the post

D Multiseat representation

12 Where do modern Prime Ministers have their official London home?

A 10 Downing Street

B 11 Downing Street

C 12 Downing Street

D 13 Downing Street

13 What does the Cabinet do?

A Sets the rate of taxation

B Makes important decisions about government policy

C Decides when Parliament opens

D Appoints judges

14 True or False? People who have applied for asylum and have NOT received a positive decision have the same rights to work as any other UK citizen and to receive a National Insurance number.

A True

B False

15 Where can you get foreign currency? (Select two options)

A Exchange shops

B The Passport Office

C Bureaux de change

D Duty free shops

16 What is another name for an independent school?

A Primary school

B Secondary school

C Upper school

D Public school

17 What is a TV licence?

A A permit that you must buy so that you can watch or record television programmes

B A permit that you must buy so that you can erect a television antenna on the roof of your house

C A permit that you must buy so that you can mount a satellite dish on the wall of your house

D A permit that you must buy so that you can make copies of DVDs

18 Which of these statements is correct?

A UK citizens have to carry identity (ID) cards

B UK citizens do not have to carry identity (ID) cards

19 What is NARIC?

A Northern Area Resource Information Centre

B National Academic Recognition Information Centre

C Nationwide Assessment Referencing Investigation Centre

D National Assessing Recruiting Interview Committee

20 True or False? Jobs that are advertised on supermarket notice boards and in shop windows are usually part-time and low paid.

A True
B False

21 What is the maximum number of hours that a child can work at a job in any school week?

A 12 hours
B 18 hours
C 20 hours
D 38 hours

22 True or False? Council tax does NOT apply to rented properties.

A True
B False

23 When was there a Catholic plot to kill the Protestant king, the failure of which is now celebrated each year?

A 1505
B 1605
C 1705
D 1805

24 True or False? Women are entitled to maternity leave only after they have completed their first year in the job.

A True
B False

Test 7

For the answers to test 7 see page 192.

1 When did Parliament pass new laws giving women the right to equal pay?
A 1920s and 1930s
B 1940s and 1950s
Ç 1960s and 1970s
D 1980s and 1990s

2 What information was NOT collected as part of the 2001 census?
A Ethnicity
B Pet ownership
C Housing
D Health

3 What fraction of the population are young people up to the age of 19?
A Almost one-fifth
B Almost one-quarter
C Almost one-third
D Almost one-half

4 What is the traditional way to stop young people playing a trick on you at Hallowe'en?
A Place a pumpkin lantern outside your house
B Give them sweets or chocolates
C Pretend that you are not at home
D Call the police

5 How many young people go on to higher education at college or university?
A 1 in 2
B 1 in 3
C 1 in 4
D 1 in 5

6 True or False? Evidence has shown that more career opportunities have become available for women.
A True
B False

7 Who is the spiritual leader of the Church of England?
A The Archbishop of Canterbury
B The Monarch
C The Pope
D The Lord Chancellor

8 Which of the following documents is NOT normally accepted by a bank as proof of identity when opening an account?
A A benefits book
B A recent gas bill
C A letter from a friend
D A Home Office immigration document

9 What service is the local authority legally required to provide?

A Water

B Electricity

C Housing

D Gas

10 What does the Prime Minister usually do if his or her party is defeated in a general election?

A The Lord Chancellor usually takes over the party

B The Prime Minister usually resigns the leadership of the party

C The Chancellor of the Exchequer usually takes over the party

D The Deputy Prime Minister usually takes over the party

11 What roles may a mayor perform? (Select two options)

A Ceremonial leader of the council

B Appointing councillors

C Effective leader of the administration

D Call a local election

12 When is the electoral register updated?

A Every year in January or February

B Every year in June or July

C Every year in September or October

D Every year in November or December

13 What is one of the main aims behind the European Union today?

A For all member states to use the euro

B For all member states to function as a single market

C For all member states to have one central Parliament

D For all member states to have one tax system

14 When was the NHS set up?

A 1948

B 1968

C 1988

D 2008

15 What is the age requirement for someone wanting to see a 'PG' classified film?

A 4 years and over

B Suitable for everyone, but parents of young children should decide if the film is suitable for viewing by them

C Children under 12 are not allowed to see or rent the film unless they are with an adult

D Children under 15 are not allowed to see or rent the film

16 What is the minimum age to drive a car?

A 16

B 17

C 18

D 21

17 True or False? Jobseeker Direct is a low-cost telephone service to help you find work.

A True

B False

18 An organisation can make a decision about whether to offer you a loan based on what TWO pieces of information about you? (Select two options)

A Your address

B Your weight

C What goods you want to buy

D Your previous credit record

19 What does income tax NOT pay for?

A Roads

B Education

C The police

D The state retirement pension

20 Just before which birthday are all young people in the UK sent a National Insurance number?

A 16th

B 17th

C 18th

D 21st

21 What is the State Pension age for men?

A 55

B 60

C 65

D 70

22 What may learner drivers NOT do?

A Drive with L plates on the vehicle

B Drive with someone else in the car who has a full licence and is over 21

C Drive on a motorway

D Drive in the dark

23 True or False? New Deal is available only for young people and they must join as soon as they are unemployed.

A True

B False

24 Which of the following is NOT a name for a European law?

A Directive

B Framework decision

C Regulation

D Rule

Test 8

For the answers to test 8 see page 192.

1 What are Suffragettes?
A War veterans
B Women who campaigned for greater rights
C Nurses who were in the First World War
D Government officials

2 True or False? There is evidence that more men are taking responsibility for raising the family and doing housework.
A True
B False

3 What subjects are part of the national tests that children take when they are 7, 11 and 14 years old? (Select two options)
A Mathematics
B Religion
C English
D Geography

4 Which website gives information on working in the UK?
A www.ukworking.gov.uk
B www.workingintheuk.gov.uk
C www.workpermitsuk.gov.uk
D www.ukjobsguide.gov.uk

5 What percentage of the people in the United Kingdom are of white descent?
A 62%
B 72%
C 82%
D 92%

6 Where is the Scouse dialect spoken?
A Liverpool
B London
C Tyneside
D Manchester

7 In the 2001 census, what percentage of the UK population stated that they were Jewish?
A 0.5%
B 2.0%
C 5.0%
D 10.0%

8 Which of the following statements is correct?
A The members of the House of Commons are democratically elected
B The members of the House of Commons are appointed by the Prime Minister

9 When is Boxing Day?

A The day before Christmas Day

B The day after Christmas Day

C The day before New Year's Eve

D The day after New Year's Day

10 When are elections for the European Parliament held?

A Every 4 years

B Every 5 years

C Every 6 years

D Every 7 years

11 What committee do the leading Government ministers form?

A The Treasury

B The Cabinet

C The working party

D The quango

12 True or False? Civil servants have to follow the policies of the elected Government.

A True

B False

13 When is a jury used?

A To decide if someone is innocent or guilty of a serious crime

B To decide if someone is innocent or guilty of a less serious crime

C To confirm decisions made by a judge

D To choose an appropriate penalty for someone found guilty of a serious crime

14 True or False? Housing associations are independent not-for-profit organisations which provide housing for rent.

A True

B False

15 If you have problems with your neighbours, and speaking to them does not help, what should you do?

A Speak again to the neighbours about the problem

B Report the problem to the police

C Report the problem to your landlord, the local authority or housing association

D Ask a court to evict them

16 Which TWO of the following countries are members of the Commonwealth? (Select two options)

A Bangladesh

B Croatia

C Turkey

D Zambia

17 On what day of the week is Mother's Day?

A Sunday

B Monday

C Wednesday

D Friday

18 Which of the following statements is correct?

A Pregnant women should organise their ante-natal care outside work hours

B Pregnant women have a legal right to time off work for ante-natal care

19 Who should you speak to if you have health and safety concerns in your workplace? (Select two options)

A Your local MP

B Your supervisor or manager

C Your trade union representative

D The police

20 Who is responsible for organising the health treatment you receive?

A The local authority

B Your local MP

C Your GP

D A specialist

21 True or False? It is legal for your employer to force you to work more hours than has been agreed in your contract.

A True

B False

22 What percentage of the UK population today is male?

A 29%

B 39%

C 49%

D 59%

23 True or False? You must get permission to walk on any path in the countryside.

A True

B False

24 In what city will you find Stormont?

A Belfast

B Cardiff

C Edinburgh

D London

Test 9

For the answers to test 9 see page 192.

1 True or False? In the late 1960s immigrants from 'old' Commonwealth countries did not have to face strict immigration controls.

A True

B False

2 When did Parliament pass new laws prohibiting employers from discriminating against women because of their sex?

A 1920s and 1930s

B 1940s and 1950s

C 1960s and 1970s

D 1980s and 1990s

3 What percentage of children live in single parent families?

A 15%

B 20%

C 25%

D 30%

4 What exams do many young people in Scotland take at the age of 17 or 18?

A Higher/Advanced Higher Grades

B B Levels and C levels

C S Levels and SA levels

D AA and SS levels

5 True or False? There is concern about the amount of alcohol that some young people drink at one time.

A True

B False

6 What areas of Britain have declined in population over the last 20 years? (Select two options)

A The North-East

B The South-East

C The South-West

D The North-West

7 How is the electoral register updated?

A A form is sent to every household to be completed and returned

B You can collect a form to fill in if you want to be included

C No changes are made except after a general election

D Information is gathered from parents at the beginning of each new school year

8 True or False? The majority of UK residents do NOT attend religious services regularly.

A True

B False

9 When do people celebrate New Year?

A The morning of New Year's Day

B On the night of 31 December

C Straight after Christmas Day

D The day after Boxing Day

10 True or False? Several Church of England bishops sit in the House of Lords.

A True

B False

11 Which politicians are members of the Shadow Cabinet?

A Civil servants working for the Government

B Senior Opposition MPs

C Peers from the House of Lords

D The remaining MPs in Government who are not in the Cabinet

12 Where are voter registration forms available from? (Select two options)

A At www.electoralcommission.org.uk

B At your local police station

C Your local council registration election office

D At your local library

13 Where can you get train information (outside Northern Ireland)?

A From the National Rail Enquiry Service

B From the tourist board

C From the National Trust

D From the local authority

14 True or False? Driving away after an accident without stopping is a criminal offence.

A True

B False

15 What is the age requirement for someone wanting to see a 'U' classified film?

A Anyone aged 4 years and over

B Suitable for everyone, but their parents should decide

C Children under 12 are not allowed to see or rent the film unless they are with an adult

D Children under 15 are not allowed to see or rent the film

16 What was the treaty called that set up the European Union (EU)?

A The Treaty of Paris

B The Treaty of Brussels

C The Treaty of Strasbourg

D The Treaty of Rome

17 Which of these statements is correct?

A A number of places on a school's governing body are reserved for parents

B A school's governing body is only made up of councillors and teachers

18 What time do pubs that have not applied for an extended licence usually close in the evening?

A 7.30pm

B 9.00pm

C 10.00pm

D 11.00pm

19 Where can you NOT get help and advice on problems at work?

A The Jobcentre

B The Citizens Advice Bureau

C A law centre

D The National Advisory, Conciliation and Arbitration Service (Acas)

20 How do employees pay their National Insurance contributions?

A It is automatically deducted from their pay by their employer every week or month

B They pay in full at the end of each year

C They pay each week at the post office

D They pay in full at the beginning of each year

21 What are redundancy payments based on?

A Skills

B Work experience

C Length of time you have been employed

D Marital status

22 What TWO sources of advice can you go to for more information on the minimum wage? (Select two options)

A The Inland Revenue

B Department of Communities and Local Government

C Central Office of Information Directgov website

D National Minimum Wage helpline

23 From October 2007, what organisation have the Commission for Racial Equality, the Equal Opportunities Commission and the Disability Rights Commission become?

A The Racial Equal Rights Commission

B The Commission for Equality and Human Rights

C The Disability and Racial Equality Commission

D The Commission for Racial Equality, Equal Opportunities and Disability Rights

24 True or False? Newspapers carry both facts and opinion pieces.

A True

B False

Test 10

For the answers to test 10 see page 192.

1 True or False? Women in Britain have the same access as men to promotion and better paid jobs.
A True
B False

2 Which of these statements is correct?
A People over 16 years of age may choose to study at colleges of further education
B People under the age of 16 often study at colleges of further education

3 True or False? There are concerns about the safety of children who work illegally or without proper supervision.
A True
B False

4 Which religion celebrates Hanukkah?
A Muslim
B Hindu
C Jewish
D Christian

5 True or False? Both Houses of Parliament have public galleries.
A True
B False

6 When can the census information be freely accessed by the general public?
A After 10 years
B After 50 years
C After 75 years
D After 100 years

7 In what part of the UK is the Welsh language widely spoken?
A Cornwall
B Northern Ireland
C Wales
D Scotland

8 What exams do most young people in England take at age 16?
A CGSE (Certificate of General Secondary Education)
B SEGC (Secondary Education General Certificate)
C GSEC (General Secondary Education Certificate)
D GCSE (General Certificate of Secondary Education)

9 True or False? Your CV contains your employment history.
A True
B False

10 What event celebrates Guy Fawkes night?

A Fireworks are set off
B Street parties are held
C Schools are closed for the day
D A parade is held through the streets

11 What is the cut-off date on the annual voter registration form?

A 15 May
B 15 July
C 15 October
D 15 December

12 Where does the Scottish Parliament meet?

A Holyrood
B Stirling Castle
C Aberdeen
D Glasgow

13 True or False? The UK is a member of the Commonwealth.

A True
B False

14 Where is the European Commission based?

A Paris
B Brussels
C Strasbourg
D Luxembourg

15 What is the name of financial help that young people from families with low incomes can get when they leave school at 16 to help them with their studies?

A Young Person's Education Allowance
B Education Maintenance Allowance
C Education Help Scheme
D Financial Help System

16 True or False? All state, primary and secondary schools in England, Wales and Northern Ireland follow the National Curriculum.

A True
B False

17 How old must you be to drink wine or beer with a meal in a hotel or restaurant?

A 14 or over
B 16 or over
C 18 or over
D 21 or over

18 True or False? Entrance to many museums and art galleries is free.

A True
B False

19 What is the speed limit for cars and motorcycles in built-up areas?

A 30 miles per hour
B 40 miles per hour
C 60 miles per hour
D 70 miles per hour

20 Between what ages can women claim Jobseeker's Allowance?

A 18-60
B 18-65
C 21-60
D 21-65

21 Which of the following organisations can give you information and advice on setting up your own business? (Select two options)

A A bank
B Your local library
C Business Link
D The Trades Union Congress

22 Which statement is NOT true?

A An employee can be dismissed immediately for serious misconduct at work

B Anyone who cannot do their job properly should be given a warning by their employer

C Anyone who has been given a warning by their employer and has not improved can be dismissed

D Anyone who has poor attendance at work can be dismissed immediately

23 Who is responsible for checking the hours and conditions for working children?

A The local authority

B Pressure groups

C Trade unions

D The Citizens Advice Bureau

24 Which of the following statements is true?

A All areas of the UK have a single local authority

B Some areas of the UK have district and county councils rather than a single local authority

Study tips

Here is a summary of study techniques that may help you revise the information you need to learn to pass the Life in the UK Test. Try a variety of techniques to find what works best for you.

The information you need to learn to pass the Life in the UK Test is not difficult to understand. It is designed to provide you with knowledge that will help you settle into this country. However, simply reading through the information contained in Chapters 2 to 6 will not be enough. You should also revise the chapters so that you can remember them.

GIVE YOURSELF TIME AND SPACE
You will find revision much easier if you approach it in a systematic way. Give yourself plenty of time before the test to actually learn the material. Draw up a study plan and timetable. Focus on a chapter at a time.

Find a quiet place to study. If your home has too many distractions, visit a library or learning centre where you can concentrate without being interrupted.

READ THE CHAPTERS AND MAKE NOTES
Concentrating on the practice questions alone is not a good idea. You will find it much easier to remember the facts if you understand them. The best way to do that is to see the information in context. Read through each of the study chapters carefully. Make notes and explore different revision techniques to find which ones help you remember most.

Start by making a page of notes on one topic. Condense these until they fit on a postcard. Read and re-read the postcard until you remember all of the key points. Try walking around or making gestures while you read. Speak the text out loud. Try making it into a song, or a rap or a rhyme. Investigate colour by colour-coding different areas of information. Draw connections between facts by sticking relevant images next to pieces of information. Each of these memory techniques is designed to stimulate a different part of your senses. Not all will work for you, so experiment and remember to have fun.

Test answers

This chapter contains the answers to the test questions posed in Chapters 2-6 and Chapter 8. Try not to cheat – it won't help you revise properly if you do. After you have completed a test, check your answers against those listed here. Highlight the areas you made mistakes on, then go back to the original text and learn the relevant sections again. This will give you a better chance of passing the real test.

Chapters 2–6

Chapter 2		Chapter 3		Chapter 4		Chapter 5		Chapter 6	
1	A	1	B	1	D	1	A	1	B
2	A	2	B	2	B	2	A	2	A
3	A	3	B	3	B	3	A	3	A
4	A	4	A	4	C	4	A	4	A
5	B	5	C,D	5	B	5	C,D	5	A,B
6	C,D	6	A	6	B	6	B	6	A
7	C	7	B	7	A	7	A	7	D
8	C	8	D	8	A	8	B,C	8	A
9	A	9	B	9	B	9	A	9	A
10	B,D	10	A	10	D	10	C	10	A,B
11	A	11	C	11	A	11	A	11	A
12	D	12	B	12	C	12	A	12	D
13	B	13	C	13	A	13	A	13	C
14	C	14	D	14	B	14	A	14	A
15	A	15	A	15	D	15	A,B	15	B,D
16	A	16	B	16	A	16	A	16	A
17	A	17	A	17	C	17	B	17	A
18	B	18	B	18	D	18	C	18	A
19	A	19	C	19	A	19	B	19	B
20	D	20	A	20	B	20	B	20	B,D
21	B	21	B	21	A	21	C	21	A
22	B	22	D	22	A	22	D	22	D
23	B	23	D	23	B	23	C	23	A
24	A	24	C	24	B	24	C	24	B
25	A	25	A	25	B	25	A	25	A
26	A	26	A	26	B	26	B	26	B
27	A	27	B	27	C	27	B	27	A
28	C	28	A	28	A	28	B	28	B
29	A	29	D	29	B	29	A	29	A,C
30	A	30	C	30	B	30	A	30	B

Chapter 8, tests 1–5

Test 1		Test 2		Test 3		Test 4		Test 5	
1	B	1	A	1	B	1	C	1	D
2	A	2	D	2	C	2	A	2	A,B
3	A	3	B	3	A	3	A	3	D
4	D	4	B	4	C	4	B	4	C
5	C	5	B	5	D	5	B	5	C
6	A	6	B	6	C	6	C	6	C
7	A	7	B	7	A	7	B	7	A
8	A	8	D	8	D	8	B	8	B
9	C	9	A,D	9	D	9	B,D	9	A
10	A,D	10	A	10	C	10	C	10	D
11	A	11	B	11	A,D	11	A	11	C
12	B	12	B	12	C	12	A	12	D
13	C	13	A	13	C	13	D	13	B,D
14	B	14	A	14	C	14	A	14	A
15	C,D	15	A,D	15	A	15	A	15	A
16	A	16	C	16	C	16	A	16	A,C
17	A	17	B	17	A	17	A,C	17	A,C
18	D	18	C	18	A	18	B	18	B
19	A	19	C	19	A	19	A	19	B
20	D	20	A	20	D	20	A	20	D
21	D	21	B	21	B,D	21	A	21	B
22	D	22	A	22	A	22	A	22	A,B
23	B	23	A	23	A	23	A,D	23	B,D
24	A	24	B	24	A	24	D	24	B

Chapter 8, tests 6–10

Test 6		Test 7		Test 8		Test 9		Test 10	
1	B	1	C	1	B	1	A	1	B
2	C	2	B	2	A	2	C	2	A
3	D	3	B	3	A,C	3	C	3	A
4	C	4	B	4	B	4	A	4	C
5	A	5	B	5	D	5	A	5	A
6	A	6	A	6	A	6	A,D	6	D
7	A	7	A	7	A	7	A	7	C
8	C,D	8	C	8	A	8	A	8	D
9	C	9	C	9	B	9	B	9	A
10	B	10	B	10	B	10	A	10	A
11	C	11	A,C	11	B	11	B	11	C
12	A	12	C	12	A	12	A,C	12	A
13	B	13	B	13	A	13	A	13	A
14	B	14	A	14	A	14	A	14	B
15	A,C	15	B	15	C	15	A	15	B
16	D	16	B	16	A,D	16	D	16	A
17	A	17	A	17	A	17	A	17	B
18	B	18	A,D	18	B	18	D	18	B
19	B	19	D	19	B,C	19	A	19	A
20	A	20	A	20	C	20	A	20	A
21	A	21	C	21	B	21	C	21	A,C
22	B	22	C	22	C	22	C,D	22	D
23	B	23	B	23	B	23	B	23	A
24	B	24	D	24	A	24	A	24	B

After the test

When you have passed the Life in the UK Test you are able to continue with the next stage of your journey to British citizenship. This will involve filling in forms and gathering documents and may include interviews and the seeking of legal advice. If you are successful achieving citizenship, you will be invited to a ceremony to celebrate. Once you have a passport, you will also enjoy the right to live and work in Europe.

Application procedure

Passing the Life in the UK Test is only part of the process of applying for citizenship or indefinite leave to remain within the United Kingdom. This section provides an overview of the remaining steps on your journey to citizenship and obtaining a British passport.

There are several different ways you may be able to apply for British citizenship. The route you need to take, including the type of form you must complete and the supporting documents you must produce, will be determined by several factors, including your current citizenship or nationality. These different eligibility requirements are outlined on the UK Border Agency's website: www.ukba.homeoffice.gov.uk. If, after looking at the website, you are still unsure about whether you meet the requirements for a particular application, contact the UK Border Agency direct.

UK Border Agency helplines

Immigration enquiry bureau: 0870 606 7766
Nationality contact centre: 0845 010 5200
Asylum support customer contact centre: 0845 602 1739

In addition to completing the application form that is most appropriate for your situation, you will need to fulfil a good character requirement. If you have been convicted of any crime in the last few years, or you are an undischarged bankrupt, your application is unlikely to succeed. In order to make an application, you will also need to be able to make your own decisions. This is regarded by the UK Border Agency as being of 'sound mind'. It is also sometimes referred to as the full capacity requirement.

 For further information on the fees for British citizenship or the right to abode in the UK, see the cost of applying section of the UK Border Agency website at, www.ukba.homeoffice.gov.uk

GETTING THE TIMING RIGHT

Applications for citizenship can take several months to process. You may also need some time to learn and revise the material you need to know in order to pass the Life in the UK Test. If you are staying in the UK on a temporary visa, it is a good idea to give yourself plenty of time after you have submitted your application, so your right to reside in the UK does not expire before your application has been processed. This means obtaining your application form and organising your Life in the UK Test well in advance.

After you have completed your application form and passed your Life in the UK Test, if you are currently living in the UK you will need to send them to the UK Border Agency in Liverpool, along with other supporting documentation such as proof of identity and payment for the application fee.

UK citizenship applications should be sent to:

UK Border Agency
Department 1
PO Box 306
Liverpool L2 0QN

If you are currently living in the Isle of Man or the Channel Islands, your application, documents and fee should be sent to the immigration department of the island's governing body.

If your application is refused, you do not have an automatic right to appeal. However you may write to the UK Border Agency if you believe their decision was wrong. It is a good idea to seek legal advice in such instances. For further information on where you can find legal immigration specialists, see page 8–9.

&& If you are staying in the UK on a temporary visa, it is a good idea to give yourself plenty of time after you have submitted your application, so your right to reside in the UK does not expire before your application has been processed. &&

CITIZENSHIP CEREMONY

If your application to become a British citizen is successful, you will be invited to a citizenship ceremony. This will normally take place in a register office somewhere close to where you live. If you would prefer it to happen in another location, you should include a note saying so with your application.

Once you have received your invitation, you will have 90 days to attend the ceremony. These are normally arranged for groups of people who become citizens at the same time, although you can arrange a private ceremony if you prefer. This normally incurs an additional fee. You can usually bring two guests to the group ceremony.

When you attend the ceremony, you will need to bring your proof of identity and confirm the personal details to be included on your citizenship certificate. You will be asked to make pledges of allegiance and to stand during the playing of the national anthem. If you are in Wales, you may choose to say your pledges in Welsh. In addition to swearing loyalty to your country, you will need to make an affirmation of allegiance to the Queen. If you prefer, you may do this by swearing an oath to God. Local or national public figures may also make a speech. You will be presented with your certificate of British citizenship and a welcome pack. Depending on where your ceremony takes place, you may also receive a commemorative gift.

❝ Citizenship ceremonies are normally arranged for groups of people who become citizens at the same time, although you can arrange a private ceremony if you prefer. ❞

APPLYING FOR A BRITISH PASSPORT

Once you are a British citizen, you may apply for a passport from the Home Office's Identity and Passport Service. To apply for a passport, you will need to complete an application form. You can either do this online or request an application form to be sent to you, at the Identity and Passport Service (IPS) website (www.ips.gov.uk). Large post offices also normally carry application forms and some offer a Check and Send service. This checks that you have filled in the form correctly. It takes on average two weeks to process passports submitted this way.

Citizenship ceremony oath or affirmation and pledge of allegiance

Affirmation of allegiance

I [your name] do solemnly, sincerely and truly declare and affirm that on becoming a British citizen, I will be faithful and bear true allegiance to Her Majesty Queen Elizabeth the Second, her heirs and successors, according to law.

Oath of allegiance

I [your name] swear by Almighty God that on becoming a British citizen, I will be faithful and bear true allegiance to Her Majesty Queen Elizabeth the Second, her heirs and successors, according to law.

Pledge

I will give my loyalty to the United Kingdom and respect its rights and freedoms. I will uphold its democratic values. I will observe its laws faithfully and fulfil my duties and obligations as a British citizen.

WELSH

Cadarnhau teyrngarwch

Yr wyf i, (enw), yn datgan ac yn cadarnhau yn ddifrifol, yn ddiffuant ac yn gywir y byddaf i, ar ôl dod yn ddinesydd Prydeinig, yn ffyddlon ac yn wir deyrngar i'w Mawrhydi y Frenhines Elisabeth yr Ail, ei Hetifeddion a'i Holynwyr, yn unol â'r gyfraith.

Llw teyrngarwch

Yr wyf i, (enw), yn tyngu i Dduw Hollalluog y byddaf i, ar ôl dod yn ddinesydd Prydeinig, yn ffyddlon ac yn wir deyrngar i'w Mawrhydi y Frenhines Elisabeth yr Ail, ei Hetifeddion a'i Holynwyr, yn unol â'r gyfraith.

Adduned

Rhoddaf fy nheyrngarwch i'r Deyrnas Unedig ac fe barchaf ei hawliau a'i rhyddidau. Arddelaf ei gwerthoedd democrataidd. Glynaf yn ffyddlon wrth ei chyfreithiau a chyflawnaf fy nyletswyddau a'm rhwymedigaethau fel dinesydd Prydeinig.

❝Large post offices also normally carry application forms and some offer a Check and Send service. This checks that you have filled in the form correctly.❞

The IPS recommends you apply at least six weeks before you need your passport to travel. In addition to submitting the application, you will also be invited to a passport interview. All adults who have never previously had a British passport will be invited to an interview. There is no Fast Track service for first-time adult passport applicants. The interview process takes about 30 minutes and will be carried out at one of the IPS offices in 68 locations around the UK. During the interview, you will be asked to confirm facts about yourself – information that someone trying to steal your identity may not know. For further information, contact the IPS 24-hour passport advice line.

In October 2008, the fee for a standard-sized first adult passport was £72. Jumbo passports (containing 48 pages) cost £85. Renewals, amendments and extensions also incur a fee.

IPS passport advice line

This advice line is manned by people 24-hours a day: 0300 222 0000.

LIVING IN EUROPE

Once you have a British passport, you will be free to travel overseas. As a British citizen, you will also be able to live and work in any of the 27 member states of the European Union. You will not need a work permit, although if you plan to live and work in another European state for longer than three months, you will need to apply for a residence permit within three months of arrival. As long as you are in paid employment, you will be subject to the same benefits and taxes as local employees. You will also enjoy the right to equal treatment with your fellow EU nationals.

 For further information on living and working within the European Union see the Which? Essential Guide, *Moving Abroad.*

Reforming the path to citizenship

No changes can be made to the current immigration and citizenship process without a change in Government legislation. The Home Office is currently reviewing immigration policy with a view to reforming the legislation.

During 2008 the Government published a green paper and conducted public consultations that looked into reforming immigration laws. This included creating what the Home Secretary Jacqui Smith called a 'new path to citizenship'. This would involve placing an expectation on applicants to earn the right to stay in the UK by learning English, paying tax, adhering to the country's laws and contributing to the community. Community contribution would be regarded as 'active citizenship' and could include volunteering for a charity. The Home Office has also suggested introducing a new 'probationary citizenship' stage, during which an applicant will need to demonstrate his or her commitment to the UK and to integration into British society.

A green paper is simply an outline of the Government's ideas. To become law it needs to be drafted as a bill and then passed by Parliament. The Home Office has announced an Immigration and Citizenship Bill to be placed before Parliament during the 2008-2009 session. However, even if passed by Parliament during 2009, such legislative changes will inevitably take some time to introduce.

For further information on proposed steps to reform the immigration system, see the reports *The path to citizenship: next steps in reforming the immigration system* published in February 2008 and *The path to citizenship: next steps in reforming the immigration system – Government response to consultation*, published in July 2008. Both of these documents are available as PDF downloads in the consultation papers section of the UK Border Agency's website. Alternatively, you may email the Home Office to request a printed copy.

 You may download PDFs of proposed immigration reform papers at the UK Border Agency's website, www.ukba.homeoffice.gov.uk or email requesting a printed copy to ImmigrationReform@homeoffice.gsi.gov.uk

Glossary

Accountant A qualified person or firm who helps individuals calculate how much money they or their business has earned and how much tax or VAT they are liable to pay.

Addictive substances Tobacco, alcohol or drugs that contain chemicals that can stimulate your brain into addiction.

Affirmation To make a formal and legally recognised declaration.

Allegiance Loyalty or commitment to a person, a group or a cause. Allegiance to your country is showing loyalty towards the nation.

Archbishop Most senior member of a group of bishops and leader of the Christian church in their area.

Asylum seekers People who wish to settle in a new country because their own home is too dangerous, often because of political reasons.

Bank Holiday Also known as a public holiday, this is a day when most banks, businesses and schools are closed and people may enjoy a day off.

Binge drinking The consumption of dangerously large quantities of alcoholic beverages in one session.

Birth certificate An official document, which in the UK (outside of Scotland) needs to be registered within 6 weeks of a baby's birth, registering their name, date and place of birth, and the names and occupations of their parents.

Bishop The leader of a group of Christian churches (see Archbishop).

Building society A sort of bank which traditionally manages savings and lends money to people for buying houses.

Bureaux de change Exchange shops where people may exchange one currency for another.

Burglary, Mugging Burglary usually involve stealing from someone's property, mugging involves stealing directly from an individual.

By-election An election which takes place in a single constituency between general elections when a seat in Parliament becomes free, usually because an MP has resigned or died.

Cabinet (government) A team of senior ministers who meet regularly and work closely with the Prime Minister on devising and promoting government policy.

Census (government) An official survey and count of a country's population.

Charter (government) An official statement outlining the rights and responsibilities of a given group of people (such as patients, citizens, passengers, customers etc).

Chief Whip An MP whose job it is to maintain discipline and guide voting on important bills within his or her political party in Parliament.

Civil service The politically neutral administrative arm of government.

Commonwealth of Nations A friendly alliance of countries comprising Britain and its former colonies, the majority of which accept the Queen as their nominal head of state.

Compulsory Mandatory, something that has to be done by law.

Concern To worry about a particular subject or situation.

Concession A gesture of recognition or preferential treatment.

Conflict A disagreement. An armed conflict may involve a war.

Constituency A clearly defined geographical area whose inhabitants (constituents) may vote to elect an MP as their representative in Parliament.

Constitution The normally written set of laws and principles by which a country is governed.

Controlled drugs Drugs that are legally restricted in terms of use or possession.

Convention An official agreement, made by countries or associations, about accepted behaviour.

Credit card A plastic card issued by banks and financial companies which allows people to buy goods and services before having to pay for them. The credit card company bills the person after the purchase has been made and adds interest to uncleared monthly bills.

Criminal offence An action that is against the law for which the perpetrator may be prosecuted.

Debate A discussion, often in Parliament or between interested parties, about a particular issue.

Debit card A plastic card issued by a bank or building society which people may use to buy goods or services. Unlike a credit card, the money is automatically deducted from the bank account.

Defer Put something off until a (usually agreed) later date.

Democracy A system of government whereby the leaders are accountable to the people who elected them.

Demonstrate An action taken by people who wish to raise an issue with Parliament and the public.

Devolution A system whereby powers are delegated to another group or regional government.

Dialect A form of language spoken by people in a particular area or social group.

Direct debit The automatic transfer of money from a person's account to another. This is often used by people to pay their bills on a regular basis.

Disability
A physical or mental condition that may make certain aspects of a person's life more difficult. This may include walking, talking, hearing, seeing or learning.

Discrimination The unfair treatment of a person because of their gender, race, nationality, age or disability.

Divorce The legal termination of a marriage.

Driving licence A legal document allowing the holder to drive on public roads. You must pass a test in order to gain one.

Dwelling A home, such as an apartment or house.

Electoral register The legally recognised list of registered voters in a country.

Electorate Everyone in a country or region who is entitled to vote in an election.

Eligible Allowed by law or set rules to take part in a specified action or event.

Emergency services The police, fire, ambulance and coastguard services who may be called on for help in an emergency.

Employee A worker who is paid by a business or organisation to do a job.

Environment The area in which someone or something lives. The word is also used in terms of minimising pollution and protecting natural eco-systems.

Equal rights A legal position maintaining individuals should be treated the same regardless of their gender, age, colour, religious or philosophical beliefs, or disability.

Estate agent Someone who helps owners to sell property or land in return for commission on the sale.

Ethnic minority A group of people whose race is different to that of the majority of a country's population.

Euro The currency of 12 European Union members.

European Commission The European Union's executive group.

European Union (EU) A political and economic association of 27 European nations.

Evict Make someone leave a property, usually with the support of the law.

Exchange rate The value of a currency at the point it is converted to another currency.

Faith school A school with a curriculum and governing body linked to a religion.

First past the post An election system whereby the candidate or party with the largest number of votes wins.

Free press Media that is not restricted by government.

Fund-raising The act of gathering money for a good cause or charity.

Further education College education for people beyond school age.

Gambling Risking money to try to win more money, for example in card games or by trying to guess the winner of a horse race or football match.

Gap year A year taken by students, usually before they embark on higher education, where they may work, volunteer or travel.

General election An election for all of the MPs in Parliament.

Hazards Dangers to health or well-being.

Health authority Governing bodies of the NHS in local areas.

Higher education College or university education that usually offers higher qualifications than at a further education institute.

Household All the people who live at any particular address.

House of Commons The part of Parliament where the elected MPs debate and work.

House of Lords The part of Parliament where the peers debate and work.

Housing association A not-for-profit organisation providing low-cost housing for rent.

Immigration To enter the country from abroad with the purpose of living and working here.

Income Money earned by an individual to live on, usually through a salary or wages paid in return for work.

Independent school Fee-charging private school.

Independents (politics) MPs who are not members of a main political party.

Judiciary The country's judges.

Jury A group of 12 citizens who listen to court cases and rule on whether a defendant is innocent or guilty of a crime.

Labourer Worker.

Landlord, landlady The owner of a property who lets it out.

Letting agent Estate agent who helps a landlord find a tenant.

Life Peers Members of the House of Lords.

Lord Chancellor The Minister responsible for legal affairs.

Methods of assessment Tests, exams or continuous grading that assesses a student's knowledge or progress.

Misuse Abuse a substance, such as alcohol, or use something in a reckless way.

Molestation Sexual abuse or assault.

Monarch The king or queen of a country.

Mortgage A loan used to buy a property.

MP Member of Parliament, elected by the people in his or her constituency to represent them in Parliament.

Naturalised citizen An individual who becomes a citizen of another country.

NHS National Health Service, government-funded health agency.

Oath A solemn promise or sworn declaration.

Off-licence A shop that sells alcohol to be drunk away from its premises.

On-the-spot fines A fee to be paid immediately as punishment for breaking the law.

Opposition The second largest political party in Parliament.

Patron Saint A Christian saint who is associated with a country, region or group of people.

Permit A legally binding document allowing you access to do something (for example a work permit).

Persecution Persistent harassment or ill treatment.

Pogroms Genocide based on race or religious belief.

Political asylum A safe place or country for someone to live in who has endured persecution due to their political beliefs.

Politicians People involved in creating and debating the laws of a country.

Possess To own something or have it in your keeping.

Prescription A form from the doctor to a pharmacist outlining what medicine a patient requires.

Pressure group A group of people who try to persuade the government on political issues.

Primary school A school for children between the ages of 5 and 11.

Prime Minister The leader of the political party in power and the political leader of the country.

Prohibit Formally prevent someone from doing something, usually by law.

Promotion During employment, this represents being given a more senior role, usually with greater responsibilities and higher pay.

Proportional representation A political system where political parties are assigned seats in Parliament according to their share of total votes cast.

Racism Aggressive behaviour towards someone motivated by their race.

Redundant To be made redundant is to be released from a job when there is no longer any work available.

Referendum A public vote on an issue.

Refugees People who flee their country because of war, environmental crisis or political reasons.

Residence A person's home address.

Retire To stop working, usually at the age of about 65.

Secondary school A school for children aged about 11 to 16.

Shadow Cabinet A team of senior ministers from the main opposition party, who meet regularly and work devise alternatives to government policy.

Sharia Islamic law based on the teachings of the Koran. A sharia mortgage complies with these teachings.

Sheriff (in Scotland) A judge.

Sick pay Wages earned by a worker who is unable to work due to illness.

Social security Welfare benefits paid to people who do not have enough money to live on.

Solicitor A qualified legal adviser.

Speaker (of the House of Commons) The politically neutral presiding officer who chairs debates within the House of Commons.

Tenancy The period of time a landlord lets his or her property to a tenant to live or work in.

Trade union A group of workers who join together to negotiate benefits for its members with its employer.

Treaty An official agreement between countries.

Unemployed Someone who does not have a job or work.

University A college of higher education, usually offering a degree course or similar.

Useful addresses

Advice

British Broadcasting Corporation (BBC)
Consumers' rights pages
www.bbc.co.uk/consumer/your_rights/

Childline
Telephone support for children
Tel: 0800 1111
www.childline.org.uk

Citizens Advice Bureau (CAB)
www.citizensadvice.org.uk

Criminal Injuries Compensation Authority
Tay House
300 Bath Street
Glasgow
G2 4LN
Tel: 0800 358 3601
Fax: 0141 331 2287
www.cica.gov.uk

Department for Constitutional Affairs
www.justice.gov.uk/guidance/
humanrights.htm

Directgov
Portal for all Government services
www.direct.gov.uk

Equality and Human Rights Commission

Manchester
Arndale House
The Arndale Centre
Manchester
M4 3AQ

London
3 More London
Riverside Tooley Street
London
SE1 2RG

Cardiff
3rd floor
3 Callaghan Square
Cardiff
CF10 5BT

Glasgow
The Optima Building
58 Robertson Street
Glasgow
G2 8DU

Helplines:
England 0845 604 6610
Scotland 0845 604 5510
Wales 0845 604 8810
www.equalityhumanrights.com

Parentline Plus
Telephone support for parents
520 Highgate Studios
53-79 Highgate Road
Kentish Town
London
NW5 1TL
Tel: 020 7284 5500
www.parentlineplus.org.uk

Relate Relationship Counsellors
www.relate.org.uk

The Equality Commission for Northern Ireland
Equality House
7–9 Shaftesbury Square
Belfast
BT2 7DP
Tel: 028 9050 0600
www.equalityni.org

The National Childminding Association
Tel: 0800 169 4486
www.ncma.org.uk

The Office for Fair Trading
Tel: 08457 22 44 99
www.oft.gov.uk

Victim Support
www.victimsupport.com

Which?
Campaigning and reviewing
consumer association
2 Marylebone Road
London
NW1 4DF
Tel: 020 7770 7000
www.which.co.uk

Children

The ChildcareLink
Tel: 08000 96 02 96
www.childcarelink.gov.uk

Hours and time for children at work
www.worksmart.org.uk

Education

A Curriculum for Excellence Scotland
www.acurriculumforexcellencescotland.gov.uk

Careers Scotland
Tel: 08458 502 502
www.careers-scotland.org.uk

Careers Wales
Tel: 0800 100 900
www.careerswales.com

Connexions
Tel: 080 80013219
www.connexions-direct.com

Education Maintenance Allowance (EMA)
www.dfes.gov.uk

Learndirect
Tel: 0800 100 900
www.learndirect.co.uk

Environment

National Trust
www.nationaltrust.org.uk

PDSA (People's Dispensary for Sick Animals)
www.pdsa.org.uk

Government

Parliaments

Contact your representatives
How to contact
MPs, MEPs, MSPs,
or Northern Ireland,
Welsh and London AMs.
www.writetothem.com

Isle of Man Government
Government Office
Bucks Road
Douglas
Isle of Man
IM1 3PN
Tel: 01624 686283
www.gov.im/cso/immigration

The Scottish Parliament
Edinburgh
EH99 1SP
Tel: 0131 348 5200
www.scottish.parliament.uk

The Welsh Assembly
Cathays Park
Cardiff
CF10 3NQ
Tel: 0845 010 3300 (English)
or 0845 010 4400 (Welsh)
www.wales.gov.uk

United Kingdom Parliament
The House of Commons
Westminster
London
SW1A 0AA
Tel: 020 7729 3000
www.parliament.uk

Voting

Electoral Commission
Trevelyan House
Great Peter Street
London
SW1P 2HW
www.electoralcommission.org.uk

Electoral Office for Northern Ireland
St Anne's House
15 Church Street
Belfast
BT1 1ER
Tel: 0800 4320 712 (freephone)
or 028 9044 6688
Textphone: 028 9044 6698
Fax: 028 9033 0661
www.eoni.org.uk

Information

National Statistics
www.statistics.gov.uk

Health

The Family Planning Association (FPA)
Tel: 0845 310 1334
www.fpa.org.uk

The National Childbirth Trust
www.nctpregnancyandbabycare.com

The National Health Service (NHS)
www.nhs.uk

For health practitioners
in Northern Ireland
www.n-i.nhs.uk

To find the nearest health services
in Scotland
www.show.scot.nhs.uk

For health practitioners in Wales
www.wales.nhs.uk

NHS24 – In Scotland
Tel: 08454 24 24 24
www.nhs24.com

NHS Direct Online
Tel: 0845 46 47
www.nhsdirect.nhs.uk

Housing

Northern Ireland Housing Executive
Tel: 08448 920 900
www.nihe.gov.uk

**Scottish Federation of Housing
Associations**
375 West George Street
Glasgow
G2 4LW
www.sfha.co.uk

Shelter
Tel: 0808 800 4444
www.shelternet.org.uk

Immigration

Home Office – UK Border Agency
Lunar House
40 Wellesley Road
Croydon
CR9 2BY
Tel: 0870 606 7766
www.ukba.homeoffice.gov.uk

Life in the UK Test
Tel: 0800 0154245
www.lifeintheuktest.gov.uk

States of Guernsey
Immigration & Nationality Service
New Jetty
White Rock
St Peter Port
GY1 2LL
Tel: 01481 741420
www.gov.gg/customs

States of Jersey
Customs and Immigration
Maritime House
La Route du Port Elizabeth
St Helier
Jersey
JE1 1JD
Tel: 01534 448000
www.gov.je/HomeAffairs/CusAndImm

Money

**The Association of
British Credit Unions
(ABCUL)**
Holyoake House
Hanover Street
Manchester
M60 0AS
Tel: 0161 832 3694
www.abcul.coop

The Financial Services Authority
Tel: 0845 606 1234
www.fsa.gov.uk

Independent Financial Advisers
www.unbiased.co.uk

Solicitors

Community Legal Advice
Tel: 0845 345 4 345
www.clsdirect.org.uk

Law Centres
Tel: 020 7387 8570
www.lawcentres.org.uk

Mediation UK
Alexander House
Telephone Avenue
Bristol
BS1 4BS
Tel: 0117 904 6661

The Law Society
Tel: 020 7242 1222
www.solicitors-online.com

Tax / National Insurance / Pensions

HM Revenue and Customs
Tel: 0845 300 45 55

National Insurance
Tel: 0845 91 57006
or 0845 91 55670

Self employment
Tel: 0845 915 4515

www.hmrc.gov.uk

The Pensions Advisory Service
Tel: 0845 601 2923
www.pensionsadvisoryservice.org.uk

The State Pension scheme
Helpline: 0845 606 0265
www.thepensionservice.gov.uk

Transport

National Express - Coaches
Tel: 08705 80 80 80
www.nationalexpress.com

National Rail Enquiry Service
Tel: 08457 48 49 50
www.nationalrail.co.uk

Northern Ireland Translink
Tel: 028 9066 6630
www.translink.co.uk

Scottish Citylink
Tel: 08705 50 50 50
www.citylink.co.uk

Utilities

Energywatch
Tel: 08459 06 07 08
www.energywatch.org.uk

Ofcom
Riverside House
2a Southwark Bridge Road
London SE1 9HA
Tel: 020 7981 3000
or 0300 123 3000
www.ofcom.org.uk

Transco
Tel: 0870 608 1524
www.nationalgrid.com/uk

TV Licensing
Bristol
BS98 1TL
Tel: 0870 576 3763
www.tvlicensing.co.uk

Work

Advisory, Conciliation and
Arbitration Service (ACAS)
Tel: 08457 474747
www.acas.org.uk

Jobcentre Plus
www.jobcentreplus.gov.uk

National Academic
Recognition Information Centre
(NARIC)
Oriel House
Oriel Road
Cheltenham
Gloucester
GL50 1XP
Tel: 0870 990 4088
Email: info@naric.org.uk
www.naric.org.uk

New Deal
Tel: 0845 606 2626
www.newdeal.gov.uk

Scotland: Disclosure Scotland
Helpline: 0870 609 6006
www.disclosurescotland.co.uk

The Department for Work
and Pensions (DWP)
www.dwp.gov.uk

The Home Office Criminal Records
Bureau (CRB)
Tel: 0870 90 90 811
www.crb.gov.uk

Trades Union Congress (TUC)
Congress House
Great Russell Street
London
WC1B 3LS
Tel: 0870 600 4882
www.tuc.org.uk

Training
http://jobseekers.direct.gov.uk

Volunteering and work experience

Business Link
Tel: 0845 600 9006
www.businesslink.gov.uk

Do-it
www.do-it.org.uk
www.volunteering.org.uk
www.justdosomething.net

Index

Index

Index

Which? is the leading independent consumer champion in the UK.
A not-for-profit organisation, we exist to make individuals as powerful as the
organisations they deal with in everyday life. The next few pages give you a
taster of our many products and services. For more information, log onto
www.which.co.uk or call 0800 252 100.

Which? Online

www.which.co.uk gives you access to all Which? content online and much, much more.
It's updated regularly, so you can read hundreds of product reports and Best Buy
recommendations, keep up to date with Which? campaigns, compare products, use our
financial planning tools and search for the best cars on the market. You can also access
reviews from *The Good Food Guide*, register for email updates and browse our online
shop – so what are you waiting for? To subscribe, go to www.which.co.uk.

Which? Legal Service

Which? Legal Service offers immediate access to first-class legal advice at unrivalled
value. One low-cost annual subscription allows members to enjoy unlimited legal advice
by telephone on a wide variety of legal topics, including consumer law – problems with
goods and services, employment law, holiday problems, neighbour disputes, parking,
speeding and clamping fines and tenancy advice for private residential tenants in England
and Wales. To subscribe, call the membership hotline: 0800 252 100 or go to
www.whichlegalservice.co.uk.

Which? Money

Whether you want to boost your pension, make your savings work harder or simply need
to find the best credit card, *Which? Money* has the information you need. *Which? Money*
offers you honest, unbiased reviews of the best (and worst) new personal finance deals,
from bank accounts to loans, credit cards to savings accounts. Throughout the magazine
you will find tips and ideas to make your budget go further plus dozens of Best Buys.
To subscribe, go to www.whichmoney.magazine.co.uk.

Which? Books

which?

Which? Books

Which? Books

Which? Books provide impartial, expert advice on everyday matters from finance to law, property to major life events. We also publish the country's most trusted restaurant guide, *The Good Food Guide*. To find out more about Which? Books, log on to www.which.co.uk or call 01903 828557.

" Which? tackles the issues that really matter to consumers and gives you the advice and active support you need to buy the right products. **"**

CD-ROM

To operate the CD-ROM you will need a PC with the minimum system requirements listed below. For a guide on how to use the CD-ROM, turn to pages 19-24.

Installing the program

To install the CD-ROM follow these instructions:

1 Disconnect from the internet.
2 Close all open applications.
3 Disable anti-virus software.
4 Insert CD-ROM into your drive.
5 Wait for setup to begin.
6 There will be a delay of one to two minutes for setup files to load.

Follow the instructions on the screen. Don't forget to turn your anti-virus software on again.

If the CD-ROM does not launch automatically you can start the installation manually by clicking on My Computer and then double clicking on the CD-ROM drive to launch. You can also double click on the file called Start Here on the CD-ROM. When installed the program will appear as an icon on your desktop, or you may access it via the Start menu.

How to uninstall the program

Windows Vista

1 Go to Control Panel and click on Programs and Features.
2 Click on How to Pass the Life in the UK Test CD-ROM.
3 Click Uninstall.

Windows XP

1 Go to the Start menu and click Control Panel.
2 Double click on Add or Remove Programs.
3 In the Currently installed programs box, click on How to Pass the Life in the UK Test CD-ROM and then click on Remove. If you are prompted to confirm the removal of the program, click Yes.

System requirements

Operating system – Microsoft® Windows® XP Service Pack 2 or later and Vista
Browser – Windows® Internet Explorer 6.0 or later
Memory – 64MB RAM
The program can run straight from the CD-ROM but doing so may affect its speed.